Spaces of Interaction, Places for Experience

Synthesis Lectures on Human-Centered Informatics

Editor
John M. Carroll, *Penn State University*

Human-Centered Informatics (HCI) is the intersection of the cultural, the social, the cognitive, and the aesthetic with computing and information technology. It encompasses a huge range of issues, theories, technologies, designs, tools, environments and human experiences in knowledge work, recreation and leisure activity, teaching and learning, and the potpourri of everyday life. The series will publish state-of-the-art syntheses, case studies, and tutorials in key areas. It will share the focus of leading international conferences in HCI.

Spaces of Interaction, Places for Experience
David Benyon
September 2014

Mobile Interactions in Context: A Designerly Way Toward Digital Ecology
Jesper Kjeldskov
July 2014

Working Together Apart: Collaboration over the Internet
Judith S. Olson, Gary M. Olson
November 2013

Surface Computing and Collaborative Analysis Work
Judith Brown, Jeff Wilson , Stevenson Gossage , Chris Hack , Robert Biddle
August 2013

How We Cope with Digital Technology
Phil Turner
July 2013

Translating Euclid: Designing a Human-Centered Mathematics
Gerry Stahl
April 2013

Adaptive Interaction: A Utility Maximization Approach to Understanding Human Interaction with Technology
Stephen J. Payne, Andrew Howes
March 2013

Making Claims: Knowledge Design, Capture, and Sharing in HCI
D. Scott McCrickard
June 2012

HCI Theory: Classical, Modern, and Contemporary
Yvonne Rogers
May 2012

Activity Theory in HCI: Fundamentals and Reflections
Victor Kaptelinin, Bonnie Nardi
April 2012

Conceptual Models: Core to Good Design
Jeff Johnson, Austin Henderson
November 2011

Geographical Design: Spatial Cognition and Geographical Information Science
Stephen C. Hirtle
March 2011

User-Centered Agile Methods
Hugh Beyer
2010

Experience-Centered Design: Designers, Users, and Communities in Dialogue
Peter Wright, John McCarthy
2010

Experience Design: Technology for All the Right Reasons
Marc Hassenzahl
2010

Designing and Evaluating Usable Technology in Industrial Research: Three Case Studies
Clare-Marie Karat, John Karat
2010

Interacting with Information
Ann Blandford, Simon Attfield
2010

Designing for User Engagement: Aesthetic and Attractive User Interfaces
Alistair Sutcliffe
2009

Context-Aware Mobile Computing: Affordances of Space, Social Awareness, and Social Influence
Geri Gay
2009

Studies of Work and the Workplace in HCI: Concepts and Techniques
Graham Button, Wes Sharrock
2009

Semiotic Engineering Methods for Scientific Research in HCI
Clarisse Sieckenius de Souza, Carla Faria Leitão
2009

Common Ground in Electronically Mediated Conversation
Andrew Monk
2008

Spaces of Interaction, Places for Experience
David Benyon

ISBN: 978-3-031-01078-1   print
ISBN: 978-3-031-02206-7   ebook

DOI 10.1007/978-3-031-02206-7

A Publication in the Springer series
SYNTHESIS LECTURES ON HUMAN-CENTERED INFORMATION #22
Series Editor: John M. Carroll, Penn State University

Series ISSN 1946-7680 Print   1946-7699 Electronic

Spaces of Interaction, Places for Experience

David Benyon
Edinburgh Napier University

SYNTHESIS LECTURES ON HUMAN-CENTERED INFORMATION #22

ABSTRACT

Spaces of Interaction, Places for Experience is a book about Human-Computer Interaction (HCI), interaction design (ID) and user experience (UX) in the age of ubiquitous computing. The book explores interaction and experience through the different spaces that contribute to interaction until it arrives at an understanding of the rich and complex places for experience that will be the focus of the next period for interaction design. The book begins by looking at the multilayered nature of interaction and UX—not just with new technologies, but with technologies that are embedded in the world. People inhabit a medium, or rather many media, which allow them to extend themselves, physically, mentally, and emotionally in many directions. The medium that people inhabit includes physical and semiotic material that combine to create user experiences. People feel more or less present in these media and more or less engaged with the content of the media.

From this understanding of people in media, the book explores some philosophical and practical issues about designing interactions. The book journeys through the design of physical space, digital space, information space, conceptual space and social space. It explores concepts of space and place, digital ecologies, information architecture, conceptual blending and technology spaces at work and in the home. It discusses navigation of spaces and how people explore and find their way through environments. Finally the book arrives at the concept of a blended space where the physical and digital are tightly interwoven and people experience the blended space as a whole. The design of blended spaces needs to be driven by an understanding of the correspondences between the physical and the digital, by an understanding of conceptual blending and by the desire to design at a human scale.

There is no doubt that HCI and ID are changing. The design of "microinteractions" remains important, but there is a bigger picture to consider. UX is spread across devices, over time and across physical spaces. The commingling of the physical and the digital in blended spaces leads to new social spaces and new conceptual spaces. UX concerns the navigation of these spaces as much as it concerns the design of buttons and screens for apps. By taking a spatial perspective on interaction, the book provides new insights into the evolving nature of interaction design.

KEYWORDS

Space, Place, Ubiquitous Computing, Interaction Design, User Experience (UX), Blended Space, Information Space, Digital Ecologies, Navigation, Conceptual Blending, Designing with Blends

Contents

Preface

I began thinking that using interactive systems is like being in a different space sometime in the 1990s. I was on a plane going to a conference on digital libraries in Crete when it came to me that finding things in a large digital library was rather similar to traveling through the physical world. You might be browsing around to see what was nearby, or heading directly to some particular destination. You could be skimming over the surface or drilling down to get at the details in some particular spot.

Over the last twenty years I have explored these ideas through a number of funded research projects, teaching courses to students, writing articles and exploring the issues with masters and PhD students. With this lecture, I hope to successfully pull together these ideas into a useful way of looking at the human condition in these days of pervasive and ubiquitous information and communication technologies (ICT).

Spatiality as a philosophical position has been gradually gaining ground over the same period as I have been thinking about the interaction of people in spaces. Ed Casey, the American philosopher, wrote *Getting Back into Place* in 1993 and produced the second edition in 2009. In this second edition he notes the growth of spatiality and space and place studies. Other important philosophical treatments of space, place and the human condition include Jeff Malpas's book *Place and Experience* published in 1999 and his development of Heideggerian phenomenology. Another significant contribution to spatiality and different ways of thinking about space is Tim Ingold's work including *Lines: A Brief History* (2007).

Spaces of Interaction, Places for Experience is a book on Human-Computer Interaction (HCI), interaction design (ID) and user experience (UX) in the age of ubiquitous computing, coming from a spatial point of view. In the course of the book we will explore issues of space and spatiality from a number of different types of space. We will look at physical spaces, digital spaces, information spaces, social spaces and blended spaces. We will look at how people move through different spaces and at how spatial relations can be understood in different types of space. We will look at liminal spaces, the boundaries between spaces.

And it is timely to do this. Dourish and Bell (2007) look at interaction through "the lens of infrastructure" arguing for "space as an interactional and cultural construct." Dörk et al. (2011) discuss the "information flaneur" pointing to the similarity between information searching and wandering the streets of 19th century cities. Alan Dix and his colleagues, along with others talk about "ecologies" of devices (Dix et al., 2000; Terrenghi et al., 2009). Mikael Wiberg and others talk about "information landscapes" (Stolterman and Wiberg, 2010). Most importantly the modern day philosopher Luciano Floridi discusses the idea of an "infosphere" and people as "inforgs" (Floridi, 2014) and how new technologies have brought us to the fourth great revolution in human thinking and philosophy. Just as the discovery that the Earth orbits the sun and Darwin's theory of evolution caused people to reconsider their relationships with their world so the current information revolution forces us to consider the relationships between people and their environment that now include this huge amount of readily available information.

Dourish and Bell write:

> "We refer not simply to physical infrastructures but more broadly to infrastructures as fundamental elements of the ways in which we encounter spaces—infrastructures of naming, infrastructures of mobility, infrastructures of separation, infrastructures of interaction, and so on. In so doing, we are foregrounding an interest in the cultural constructions of space, and in turn, infrastructure."

In a similar fashion, we present issues of naming and making meaning when we discuss semiotics (Chapter 2) and information spaces (Chapter 5); we look at mobility in Chapter 8 on navigation and at the social issues in Chapter 7.

In Chapter 1 we explore some of these ideas in the context of interaction design and talk about how to understand people making use of interactive systems, what level of abstraction is useful and what insight does it give us. In Chapter 2 I lay out the philosophical standing that will underpin much of the discussion. This position is that there is little point in looking at people if we define people as existing independently of their environment. A person is always somewhere and is always surrounded by stuff. People need air to breath. They often wear clothes. They use knives and forks to eat with and use long poles to knock apples off a tree. These "extensions of man" (cf. *Understanding Media* by Marshall McLuhan, 1963) allow people to extend their immediate sphere of influence. Spectacles allow me to see further. Prosthetic limbs allow para-athletes to run and jump. Cars enable me to travel faster. In this chapter we look at people and the media in which they live and how best to describe this medium to help us understand interaction.

In Chapter 3 we turn to physical spaces. How have philosophers and designers, artists and gardeners described physical spaces? What is important about the world around us—both the natural world and the built environment? What effect does the physical environment have on us as people and how we think and feel? These questions are explored through a number of phenomenological accounts of place-by-place theorists, architects and town planners.

Chapter 4 considers digital space. When I first came to computers, I understood how they worked. I understood about data and binary digits and how the data was stored and accessed. I knew about file structures and indexes and how data was transferred over networks. I knew about emails and how they were routed through different nodes on a network to make their way from my computer to someone else's. I am not sure I do any more. Chapter 4 discusses digital technologies and digital ecologies—the different configurations of devices and communications and how they work together. In Chapter 5 we look at information spaces and information architecture and how people find, or fail to find, the information that they are looking for. In Chapter 6 we turn our attention to the conceptual space of knowing and understanding and review modern theories of cognition and action and how people classify things in the world.

Chapter 7 introduces some ideas on social spaces in this context and in Chapter 8 we explore how people navigate spaces, moving from the physical world into the digital world and back again. Chapter 9 introduces blended spaces. Blended spaces are spaces where the physical world and the digital world are closely integrated and designed to provide a different sense of presence, of being in a different type of space. Some conclusions about places and experience in the blended world of ubiquitous computing are provided in Chapter 10.

An important aspect of this book is to understand what it is trying to do and what it is not trying to do. I am not a philosopher, but I do engage with philosophy. I am not classically trained on philosophical debate, but that does not stop me from having philosophical ideas. I am not a psychologist, but I do psychology. I know little about perception and little about neuropsychology, but at a conceptual level I understand how people make sense in the world.

I come at these topics from the perspective of an interaction designer and new media commentator. I come at this subject from the perspective of spaces and spatiality and how seeing people in the space of new media and ubiquitous computing provides interaction designers with new insight. Spatiality makes us think about things in terms of spatial constructs and spatial relations. We can think about how things are laid out and how close things are to one another. We can look at distance and direction and density. We can look at the ordering of objects and relations such as before and after, under and on top. We can think about how things move through spaces and how things move in spaces. We can think about perception and navigation. So the aim is to look at interaction and experience from a spatial perspective, placing people in the context of the technological world and where interaction is a fundamental primitive of the human condition.

During this exploration I lay down some challenges for philosophers. For example the current theory of the extended mind and embodied, embedded cognition argues that thinking and knowing do not happen simply inside your brain. Several philosophers use the example of a blind man's stick to question where the blind man's ability to perceive and understand is located. Andy Clark asks what is the difference in thinking between one person, Otto, who writes things in a notebook and others who remember details. Is the notebook part of Otto's thinking? However, these examples seem to me to ignore an important part of the world. I want to ask them what the stick is made of, how flexible it is and whether it is white. When Andy Clark talks about Otto's notebook I want to know how big it is, how many pages it has and what else is in it. In other words I want to know about the interaction of people with their extensions and what experiences they have as a result of using and engaging with these extensions. This is user experience and it comes from design.

The famous quotation by Plato—that in order to understand phenomena we need "to carve things up at the joints"—comes back to haunt philosophy as it has largely ignored the fundamental part that interaction has to play in cognition and experience. As interaction designers we design the extensions; we create the tasks that people have to undertake in order to do something. A designer created the blind man's stick and this fundamentally affects the blind man' experience of the world. A designer created Otto's notebook.

The second challenge for philosophy and for those working in HCI and ID is to what extent the ideas of information spaces and conceptual spaces are a metaphorical use of the idea of space and to what extent they are a literal use. If we accept that technologies provide extensions to people—that technologies are a part of the lived world—then clearly being in the world involves being in a context that includes interactive technologies. Just as we would not deny that physical spaces include the landscape, seascape and soundscape, so they include the information space, the "semioticscape," where meanings and feelings are experienced. You inhabit eBay because you want to buy some clothes and that is where the transaction takes place just as if you go to a high street store and the transaction takes place there. At some point being-in-the-world reaches out into semiotic space, whether that is the meaning attributed to a bridge over a river (to use an example from Heidegger), or the record of a credit card payment in the high street store.

Dourish and Bell conclude their paper by saying, "Finally, there is already a complex interaction between space, infrastructure, culture, and experience." In this book we explore exactly what this complex relationship is like.

Finally I would like to acknowledge the input of ideas and words into this project from Oli Mival, Shaleph O'Neil, Serkan Ayan, and Brian O'Keefe.

CHAPTER 1

Spaces of Interaction

In his introduction to *Bringing Design to Software* (Winograd, 1996) Terry Winograd asks the rhetorical question "What is Software?" And answers, "In this book, we emphasize software as a medium for the creation of "virtualities"—the world in which a user of software perceives, acts and responds to experiences" (p. xvi). He goes on to discuss other terms that people use of software, concluding that they are "all carrying the connotation that a space of existence, rather than a set of devices or images, is being designed"... and later "in this book, we approach software users as inhabitants, focusing on how they live in the spaces that designers create" (p. xvii).

Bringing Design to Software was arguably the first book on interaction design, bringing together chapters by many of the leading designers of the time (1996). It remains an excellent survey of the issues today. But it is the idea that we can consider software as a digital *space* that is of interest to us.

The term "cyberspace" had been in use since it was coined by William Gibson in his 1984 book *Neuromancer* (Gibson, 1984) and is still in popular use today to refer to the Internet and other networked information and communication technologies (ICT). Politicians refer to the war on criminals in cyberspace and others talk about the need to regulate cyberspace to stop abuse and cyber-bullying. Recently Liam Bannon has focused on spaces in his Interactions essay on reimagining HCI (Bannon, 2011).

In this book we will take a spatial view of Human-Computer Interaction (HCI), interaction design (ID), and user experience (UX). This means that we use the concepts of spaces to think about interactive experiences. Spaces lead us to think of places, ecologies and environments. We can think about insides and outsides, about boundaries and horizons. We can think about moving through spaces, about paths. We can think about landmarks and districts. We can think about spatial relations such as on and off, in and out, in front and behind. Thinking spatially makes us think about layout, topology, density, direction and distance.

The idea is not to use space as a metaphor for what goes on in HCI, ID and UX; it is to bring concepts of spatiality and of people being in spaces to understand the design of user experience from a different perspective. We will explore the nature of experience in an age of ubiquitous and pervasive computing, when information spaces such as Facebook, Google and the Huffington Post are an integral part of those experiences. This change of perspective is important as by using concepts of space to look at experiences, we see people as being in social and technological environments. We do not carve up experience in terms of humans, computers and their interactions. We look at user experience as a whole and interaction design as the design for those experiences.

1.1   INTERACTION DESIGN

Interaction design is about designing interactive systems, products, spaces and services for people. It is a very particular discipline. It shares characteristics with all design activities in that it is concerned with "shaping some medium to fit human purposes," but interaction design has its own characteristics. Mitch Kapor captures the issues well (Kapor in Winograd, 1996).

"What is design? It's where you stand with a foot in two worlds—the world of technology and the world of people and human purposes—and you try to bring the two together."

Design is rarely a straightforward process and typically involves much iteration and exploration of both requirements (what the system is meant to do and the qualities it should have) and design solutions. Both problem and solution need to evolve during the design process; rarely can you completely specify something before some design work has been done. Design is very much a craft that draws upon both engineering and creative approaches. The famous design commentator Donald Schön has described design as a "conversation with materials," by which he means that in any type of design, designers must understand the nature of the materials that they are working with (Schön, 1983). Design works with and shapes a medium; in our case this medium centers on interactive systems.

Interactive system is the term we use to describe the technologies that interaction designers work with. This term is intended to cover components, devices, products and software systems that are primarily concerned with processing digital content. The term "digital content" refers to all the digital assets (movies, music, photos, animations, graphical images, text messages, e-mails, spreadsheets, slide shows, etc.) that an interactive device contains or provides access to. Digital content also includes the functions that an interactive system can provide. For example some interactive devices will let people view photos but not change them, whereas others will let people edit the photos and upload them to a photo sharing website. Other interactive systems will provide functions for people to control other devices. When we talk about digital content, we need to consider both the assets and the functions that an interactive system allows people to access and process.

Interactive systems are things that deal with the transmission, display, storage or transformation of digital content that people can perceive. They are devices and systems that respond dynamically to people's actions. How quickly they respond to people's actions is an important aspect of interaction. My garden is an interactive system, because I can change it and shape it and plant flowers in it, but it responds to my actions only after months or years. Most interaction design is concerned with products and systems that react quickly to people's actions. However, an interactive service such as a pension plan may react over longer periods to any user actions.

Of course interactive components are increasingly being included in all manner of other products (such as clothes, buildings and cameras). So interaction designers need to think beyond the immediate use of an interactive system and consider the wider physical and social settings in which the interaction will happen, how interactions change over time and locations and how content is experienced through different devices.

A further challenge for interaction designers is to deal with the fact that people are flexible, creative and resourceful, but interactive systems tend to be rigid and intolerant of errors. People and interactive systems speak different languages. People have intentions, desires and feelings. They want to get on with doing things and having positive experiences. Interactive systems, on the other hand, need to be given strict instructions. So designers need to produce interfaces to interactive systems that enable people to shape and achieve their goals and aspirations. These interfaces include all the physical, perceptual and conceptual touchpoints that there are between people and the content that is contained in, or is accessible by, the interactive system.

The rapid exchanges between people's actions and the systems' responses, and how these contribute to people's experiences, and how they achieve their goals is one side of the activity of interaction design. But of course people can only form desires and aspirations given their knowledge of the opportunities offered by the current and imagined situations and that includes their understanding of technologies and the content that is available. Thus interactive systems provide opportunities for people to plan activities and to undertake actions. In their turn the activities set requirements for technologies to fulfill.

Interaction design is about creating the media in which people engage with digital content—perceiving it, playing with it, consuming it, producing it, manipulating it, communicating it. If architecture focuses on where we live and work and clothing design on what we wear, then interaction design focuses on what we do with digital content. And just as there are many social, political and technological issues with architecture and clothing, so there are with digital content.

1.2   PACT: A CONSTRUCT FOR UNDERSTANDING INTERACTION

We conceptualize interaction as a relationship between four elements: people, activities, contexts and technologies (Pact). For example, a grandmother sets the controls on her intruder alarm in the hallway of her house. In this case the P (people) is the grandmother, the A (activities) is setting the controls on an intruder alarm, the C (context) is her hallway (and all the myriad other aspects of context, such as her being on her own, it is late at night, she has had a certain level of education and has past experiences of setting the alarm, and so on, and so on) and the T (technologies) is the intruder alarm itself. Another example might be "a number of teenagers traveling to meet up, arrange to meet at a café using text messages." Here the P is the group of teenagers and the individual teenagers, the A is arrange to meet up, the C is traveling (whether on a bus, walking or cycling and all the other aspects) and the T is the mobile phones and the network and the text messages themselves.

Pact is a useful way to keep focused on the wide range of issues that are the concern of interaction design. It reminds us that people are always in an environment that consists of contexts and technologies. It reminds us that people are trying to do things; they are engaged in activities. It is also useful because we can "look inside" a Pact and see two key relationships. The interaction between the people and technology (P and the T) is the interface, or user interface, in past times called the human-computer interface. Issues here concern ensuring a good fit between the technology and the capabilities of people; for example by making a button on a smartphone big enough to press, or some content on a website big enough to read. The second relationship—between the P&T taken together and the activities and contexts—highlights the effectiveness and overall experience of a particular P&T for undertaking some activity in context. For example, the grandmother in the previous example may have difficulty finding and pressing the appropriate button to set the alarm. She might not understand the different combinations of settings that are available (i.e., she is not aware of all the digital content). So whereas the technology might be fine for the salesman who sold her the alarm, it may not be a satisfactory experience of the particular person in a particular context.

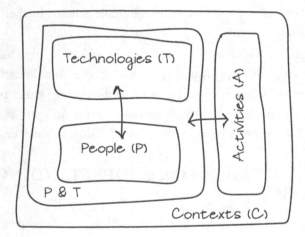

Figure 1.1: Pact.

But of course it is much more complex than this. At any one time there will be many, many Pacts going on, for individuals and for groups of people. As I am writing this, interacting with a keyboard and mouse, clicking and double clicking, swiping and scrolling, moving the mouse pointer, clicking to position it, typing some more letters, deciding whether to use the back button to correct a mistake, or whether to highlight the word and cut it, or just type the correction over it, or taking advantage of a pop-up suggestion by the spell checker. I hear a sound that indicates an e-mail has arrived and in the corner of my eye I see the message pop up, so decide whether or not to answer it. I am aware of people putting up scaffolding in the distance. I have taken my jacket off and it is hanging on the back of a chair. I can see the reflection of the windows in my screen....

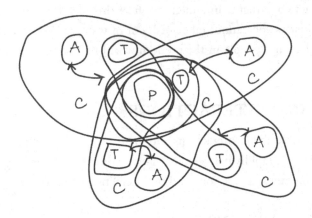

Figure 1.2: Multiple Pacts.

So, there are all these combinations of Pacts going on and evolving over time. This is the environment that we are in and if you want to understand human experiences you can't take us out of our environments! John Dewey, a philosopher writing in the 1930s, said, "life goes on in an environment; not merely in it, but because of it, through interaction with it" (Dewey, 1934). Maurice Merleau-Ponty, writing in the 1960s said, "The world is not what I think, it is what I live through" (Merleau-Ponty, 1962).

As we will see in Chapter 2, people are always in this Pact environment; or rather people are always in multiple Pacts that are going on simultaneously. This is the medium in which we exist as people. And it has changed since these philosophers were writing as now our world includes digital content and interactive systems. Traditional philosophy almost always puts the human in the foreground as the object of interest. Philosophers such as Rene Descartes, writing in 1637, focused on the person as the basic unit of analysis. His famous dictum *Cogito ergo sum* (I think therefore I am) led to a period in philosophy where people were seen as separated from their environment. This view has continued to this day with philosophers and psychologists trying to understand what goes on in people's heads. However, starting from the beginning of the 20th century, a different philosophy began to emerge. In the U.S. this was known as pragmatism and is represented by the work of Charles Sanders Peirce, William James and John Dewey. In Europe, Edmund Husserl, Martin Heidegger and Maurice Merleau-Ponty (amongst others) pursued a philosophy known as phenomenology. This recognized that in order to understand things and understand how people think and act, you need to understand the whole, the "essence" in Husserl's terms, "the things them-selves" (Husserl, 1970).

In the 21st century, this phenomenological view of action and cognition has gained a lot more influence. The Pact construct is intended to reflect this idea that you cannot take people out of their environment, just as you cannot take a fish out of water and expect it to continue living as a fish. We want to understand people in the modern world that consists of many things including interactive technologies and digital content. Pact will help us focus on this.

1.3   DESCRIBING INTERACTIONS

There are many ways of describing interactions and many levels of description that need to be con-sidered. Designers will move rapidly between focusing on details and focusing on the bigger picture. They will focus on momentary interactions and on interactions over time.

1.3.1   MICROINTERACTIONS

There are microinteractions concerned with fine-grained details of a single "use case." Activities such as "turn my smartphone's ring tone off," "log on to my account," "take a picture" or "post a tweet on Twitter" are examples of microinteractions. Dan Saffer talks about these in his book of the same title (Saffer, 2013). Microinteractions consist of a trigger, a set of rules for determining what the system does next, feedback to let people know what the rules have done and then loops and modes that determine what happens over time and what happens if circumstances change, e.g., there is an interruption to the process. For Saffer, microinteractions are a philosophy for design, concentrating on the details of interactions and aiming to keep interactions simple and clearly focused. Do one thing well. Of course interactive systems do rapidly become much more complex than just doing one thing, so another part of the philosophy is to consider the whole interactive product or system as a series of microinteractions.

Dan Saffer talks about how well-designed microinteractions can become product "signature moments." Think of the "Like" button on Facebook, the one-click order on Amazon, the "silence my iPhone" button or the unusual and novel "click wheel" interaction on the original iPod. These well-designed, simple and effective controls can define a product and create satisfying and engaging interactions.

1.3.2   SYSTEM FEATURES

At another level of detail we can consider how the microinteractions are put together into system features. This might include the overall layout of a screen and the relationships between the text, icons and other features. Common interaction patterns can be defined. For example, the palette on Microsoft products such as PowerPoint, or the inspector on Apple products such as Keynote, package a number of microinteractions into a coherent collection. Menus demonstrate another method for packing interactions into larger units. The design of screen displays and web pages is another way of collecting together microinteractions, and here we might look to an expert on graphic layout such as Aaron Marcus (2014).

1.3.3   TASKS

Interactions may be described at the level of tasks, and in the past considerable effort has been devoted to task analysis (e.g., Diaper and Stanton, 2003). Task analysis concerns the relationships between the P, C and T of Pact taken together and the domain in which the Pact is happening. A domain is a sphere of activity such as setting intruder alarms or meeting up with friends. The assumption is that the PCT system wants to achieve a certain state of the domain. This is the goal of the PCT system (such as "intruder alarm set," or a "successful meeting with friends"). In order to achieve this goal the PCT system will have to undertake some tasks. The tasks are prescribed by the technology and consist of actions undertaken in some sequence that may require some actions to be repeated a number of times. Thus the focus of a task analysis of some experience is on how effective a particular Pact is at bringing about changes in a domain.

Recipes are good examples of tasks. Suppose you have the goal of having some soup and croutons for lunch. This could be expressed at the task level as make the soup (task 1) and make the croutons (task 2). Task 1 is then expressed in terms of the actions: fry onions (action 1); add vegetables (action 2); add stock (action 3); cook for 20 minutes (action 4); liquidize (task 5). Note that we describe the actions in a particular sequence. Tasks are sequences of actions. We can elaborate on the tasks, by including iterative actions (e.g., fry onions and continue to fry until soft) and optional actions (e.g., if you would like a smooth soup, liquidize, otherwise leave out this action). Tasks for some people will be actions for others, and vice-versa. For example if the recipe says "make a roux," some people will understand that as a simple action, whereas others will see it as a major task; "how do I make a roux?"

By coming up with a particular design, designers create tasks for people.

1.3.4   SERVICE DESIGN

Another view of interactivity is to look at interactions over a period of time and over different devices. Sometimes called the "customer journey" the focus here is on the UX not as a microinteraction, but as a series of actions over a period of time. Experiences such as taking a plane trip or having holiday will require multiple interactions over time, often using different devices. Interactions with Facebook, for example go on over many years. People access services from different devices at different times, so the whole UX needs to consider the nature of these different "touchpoints" or service moments and how they come together into a coherent experience.

When considering service design, designers need to think about how the user comes to know about the service in the first place and how this might involve designing for social media such as Facebook or Twitter, or designing TV advertising or poster promotions. Then the service needs to support the person planning their activities, undertaking their activities, revising their activities and revisiting their activities. The service needs maintain consistency across devices and across episodes in the service so that people can interrupt a service, come back to it later and be in the right place. Service design is about experiences over time coming together into a coherent whole.

1.3.5   THE PACT ELEMENTS

Designers might focus on the person-technology relationship (P-T) in a Pact. This is commonly called the user interface. Here the designer will need to consider the actions that a user will need to undertake, the responses that the system will provide and the overall aesthetics and look and feel of the interaction. Of course they will almost always be many layers to this, and many media involved. On another occasion designers will want to focus on the person-technology system taken as a whole and the relationship between the people-technology system and the activities and contexts (P-T and A-C). For example a designer might be attending to how effective an app on a smartphone is for the activity of finding a particular type of shop in a strange city.

On other occasions designers will attend to the different elements of Pact. They might focus on the people in a Pact, what they are thinking, how they are feeling and what they understand, or how they conceive of the whole Pact situation that they are in. They might focus on what happens to the interaction in a particular context. They might focus on the nature of the different technologies and the suitability of a particular technology for a particular activity, or how the nature of a technology might change a task or one of the microinteractions. They might focus on the activity that people are engaged with and how a service could be designed to support a particular activity.

1.3.6   LEVELS OF ABSTRACTION

All these different views on interactions and interactivity can lead to confusion and muddled thinking. So it is essential that we identify the level of abstraction that we are working at. Luciano Floridi (2008) describes the concept of a level of abstraction in great detail and uses it as an essential piece of his philosophy of information and telepresence. In the case of interactivity there are different levels of abstraction for microinteractions, tasks, services and for different views of these focusing on the user interface, usability, UX and so on.

The idea of attending to levels of abstraction has been important in many forms of analysis of interactive and non-interactive systems. Systems theory (Checkland, 1999) is an approach to understanding the world recognizing that the concept of a system can be applied to all manner of things from oceans to atmospheres to business organizations and interactivity. A system is a more or less complex object that is recognized, from a particular perspective (or level of abstraction), to have a relatively stable, coherent structure. Systems contain subsystems and are contained within super-systems (or environments). Systems interact with other systems. Systems interact with their environments, with their subsystems and with other systems at the same level of abstraction.

Simply put the idea of a level of abstraction is to be explicit about the perspective from which an observer looks at a system. Floridi describes this in terms of the variables that are used in a discourse and the values that these variables can take. So to understand information one needs to understand the level of abstraction and to understand the sense of presence one needs to know the level of abstraction. Similarly to understand interaction we need to understand the level of abstraction that we are talking about. For example I can describe an action on a computer screen as "open the document called Doc1" or perhaps "double click on the icon on the screen labeled 'Doc1'," but for the programmer the icon is simply a number of pixels at a certain location and a double click is depressing and releasing a mouse button within a certain period of time.

1.4   INTERACTION AND USER EXPERIENCE

Just as we want to treat the Pact elements as a whole in order to focus on interaction as the object of study, so we want to treat the user experience (UX) as a whole. The UX is created from the Pact elements and it will be a good UX if these elements are harmonized with respect to some domain. So an iPhone may provide a great UX most of the time, but it is not very good if you are wearing gloves on a cold winter's day. Considered from the user's point of view, UX is a felt experience. It is emotional, physical, thoughtful and meaningful. Often it is social and it may be useful. UX may be a quality of a moment or a short or long period.

Contributions to an understanding of designing for UX come from many different areas. Nathan Shedroff published a very engaging book called *Experience Design* (Shedroff, 2009) and John McCarthy and Peter Wright explore the wider issues of experiences through their book *Technology as Experience* (McCarthy and Wright, 2004) and *Experience-centered Design* (Wright and McCarthy, 2010), drawing on the philosophy of the American pragmatist philosopher John Dewey. Patrick Jordan and Don Norman have both published books on the importance of emotion in design and designing for pleasurable experiences (Jordan, 2003; Norman, 2004) and others talk about "ludic" design, "hedonomics" and "funology" (Blythe, et al., 2006). Work on aesthetics has a long history and has recently been applied to interactive systems design (Hassenzahl, 2010).

UX design is about recognizing that interactive products and services do not just exist in the world, they affect who we are. They influence our culture and identity. As Dewey said many years ago "experience is the irreducible totality of people acting, sensing, thinking, feeling and meaning-making including their perception and sensation of the artifact in context" (quoted in (McCarthy and Wright, 2004). UX is concerned with all the qualities of an experience that really pull people in—whether this is a sense of immersion that one feels when reading a good book, or a challenge one feels when playing a good game, or the enjoyment one gets from using an engaging smartphone app. UX is concerned with all the qualities of the interactive experience that make it memorable, satisfying, enjoyable and rewarding (or not).

In their treatment of technology and experience, McCarthy and Wright highlight the need to take a holistic and pragmatic approach to UX. They argue that experiences have to be understood as a whole and cannot be broken down into their constituent parts, because experience lies in the relations between the parts. Interactivity involves the combination of people, technologies, activities and the social and cultural contexts in which the interaction happens (which is Pact, of course). Designers need to consider the combination of these elements and strive to achieve a harmonious combination.

Experiences, therefore, cannot really be designed. Designers can design *for* experience, but it is individuals and groups who have the experience. However, designers can be sensitive to the characteristics that create a good experience and can draw upon knowledge of designing for engagement, fun, pleasure and aesthetics.

1.4.1   ENGAGEMENT

Engagement is about ensuring that the interaction flows. Shedroff (2009) identifies five key features of engagement: identity, adaptivity, narrative, immersion and flow. Identity is needed for authenticity in the experience and expression of the self. The authenticity of an experience is about ensuring experiences are real, or realistic, and consistent. Adaptivity is to do with change and personalization and with changing levels of difficulty, pace and movement. Narrative is to do with telling a good story, with convincing characters, plot and suspense. Narrative is not just about fiction, however. Good narrative is just as important for a company's promotional video, a lecture on interaction design, a menu structure on a mobile phone or any other design problem. Immersion is the feeling of being wholly involved within something, with being taken over and transported somewhere else. You can get immersed in all manner of things (such as reading a book) so immersion is not about the medium; it is a quality of the design. Finally, flow is the sense of smooth movement, the gradual change from one state to another.

Flow is an important concept introduced by the psychologist Mihaly Czikszentmihaly. A medium is engaging if it draws the person in, if it seems to surround the activity, if it stimulates the imagination. Malcolm McCullough in his book *Abstracting Craft* (McCullough, 1998) argues that an engaging medium allows for continuity and variety, for "flow" and movement between many subtle differentiations of conditions. The medium can take many slightly different positions along a spectrum that are just discernible by a person. Think of the way the lights go down in a cinema just before the movie starts. The sense of anticipation, satisfaction and being drawn-in is created by the just discernible change in lighting. In another one of his books, McCullough writes: "Flow needs contexts. A river, for example, needs riverbanks otherwise it spreads out in every direction until it becomes a brackish swamp…. Flow is the sense of engagement that emerges, between boredom and anxiety, when practiced abilities are applied to challenges that are just about manageable." (McCullough, 2005)

1.4.2   ENJOYMENT

Product designers have long been concerned with building in pleasure as a key marketing point. Pleasure is a focus for many design situations that were once much more dominated by the more functional aspects of usability. Patrick Jordan's book *Designing Pleasurable Products* argues that designing for pleasure can be as important as ensuring that an interactive device is usable. Jordan describes pleasure as being "the condition of consciousness or sensation induced by the enjoyment or anticipation of what is felt or viewed as good or desirable; enjoyment, delight, gratification." In the context of interactive devices or products, designing for pleasure contributes to "emotional, hedonistic and practical benefits" (Jordan, 2003).

Jordan's approach draws heavily on the work of Lionel Tiger, an anthropologist who has developed a framework for understanding and organizing thinking about pleasure. He discusses the physical aspects of pleasure, the social aspects, psychological aspects and the importance of personal values to providing a good UX. Don Norman (2004) also highlights the importance of physical, psychological and ideological issues that impact on the pleasure we take in having some interactive experiences.

The experience of games' designers can also highlight what makes an experience engaging. In interaction design there has been much discussion about principles of "gamification" and how design ideas developed for playing computer games can be introduced to make other interactive experiences more enjoyable. Nicole Lazzaro (2012) is a games designer who has developed the "four keys of fun" theory that draws the link between fun, engagement and emotion. She identifies five ways that emotions impact user experience. Emotions create strong shifts in internal sensations that let people enjoy things. Emotions also help gamers to focus effort and attention and are central to decision making. Emotions increase appeal to enhance performance and are important for motivation and attention to help learning. She goes on to distinguish hard fun, from easy fun, to serious fun and people fun.

1.4.3   AESTHETICS

Aesthetics is a large area of study concerned with human appreciation of beauty and how things are sensed, felt and judged. Aesthetics takes us into the world of artistic criticism and the philosophy of art itself. The perennial debate here is whether aesthetics can ever be inherent in something, or whether "beauty is in the eye of the beholder."

Hassenzahl (2010) discusses UX in terms of pragmatic attributes and hedonic attributes. Hedonic attributes are concerned with the emotion and enjoyment of a particular experience. Pragmatic attributes are concerned with effectiveness and efficiency. He argues that emotion is at the heart of experience because emotion, cognition, motivation and action are all intrinsically interwoven. He identifies the different levels of abstraction that are to be considered in UX design: motivational goals—how do you want to be—goals concerned with what you need to do and those concerned with how you do it. He summarizes the situation "in experience design we use functionality, content, presentation and intention as materials to shape experiences." Certainly, there is more than traditional usability at work in people's judgments of quality of interactive systems, but at times people will rate usability as most important. Content, services and brand are also factors to be taken into consideration.

1.4.4 INTERACTION AND UX OVER TIME

John Zimmerman and Jodi Forlizzi from Carnegie Mellon University have been researching and developing ideas on interaction design for a number of years. Zimmerman (2009) looks at the feelings that people have for products and the ways in which the products take on meanings for them. From his analysis he arrived at six "framing constructs" that captured important elements of product attachment. *Role engagement* concerns support for the different roles that people play in their lives. It arises from the observation that people have to switch roles depending on the context such as the time of day, or relationship required for a particular activity. *Control* concerns empowering people, giving them control over the product. This could be control over the "look and feel" of the product, personalizing it to their tastes, or it could be control over the functionality of the product. *Affiliation* concerns how people develop feelings for a product by ensuring the product meets a real need for them. *Ability and bad habit* is a construct concerned with enhancing people's abilities and preventing them making mistakes or engaging in their bad habit. In addition to these short-term framing constructs, Zimmerman and Forlizzi look at how *long-term goals need supporting* as well as short-term functions. People build their attachment by recognizing the product supports their long-terms goals. Zimmerman describes this in terms of *ritual*, and how important it is to support our daily routines and how the product fits in with important ritual aspects of the person's life.

In Karapanos et al. (2009) they, along with other colleagues, explore some of these issues. Drawing upon the ideas of social and cultural adoption they identify three stages in the uptake of technologies by people. Commodification is the early stage as designers and users develop the identity of a product. Gradually people can see how a product could fit into their lives and they appropriate and incorporate it into their ways of being, finally resulting in conversion when the product is a natural part of social interactions. They then undertake an empirical study to see how far these ideas can be used to understand the development of UX over time. They conclude with a model of the "temporality of experience" that shows how people move through phases of having an experience based upon three forces of familiarity, functionality and emotional involvement. The different aesthetic qualities of the experience (hedonic and pragmatic) interact in different ways with issues of utility and ease-of-use at different stages of the process. They recommend that designers focus on designing for meaningful mediation, designing for daily rituals and designing for the self.

1.5   SUMMARY

Spaces of interaction are made up of people undertaking activities using technologies in contexts, Pact. There are many levels of description and many levels and types of interaction. People interact over time, across devices and with other people. People have different motivations, feelings and intentions for doing things. They interact with multiple Pacts simultaneously and move between different experiences as they change their goals and derive meanings from interactions.

Interaction design is about creating user experiences aiming to provide an engaging, enjoyable and meaningful experience for people in both the short and longer term. This includes aesthetics, pleasure and emotional engagement in terms of both the product and the service provided. In particular it is important to consider experiences at a physical, behavioral and social level and in terms of the meanings people derive from their experiences. With interaction increasingly concerned with the overall service experienced through different devices and different times and with the interactive experience lasting over long periods of time, designers need to focus not just on immediate interactions, but also on the long-term experience.

It is these spaces of interaction that we need to design for because it is within these experiences that people inhabit their worlds.

CHAPTER 2

The Medium of Interaction

Marshall McLuhan, a writer in the 1960s, famously said "the medium is the message," by which he meant that media such as radio, TV, clocks, electric light, photographs or wheels were not simply things that carried content (messages); the medium is the content. Many people still see a medium as something that carries meaning from one place to another, the so-called conduit metaphor of communication, but for McLuhan and others it is rather different. He saw people as immersed in media that enabled and empowered people to reach out and engage with new activities. Indeed the subtitle of his book *Understanding Media* is "*The Extensions of Man*" (McLuhan, 1963).

This is the idea behind Pact. People are surrounded all the time by media (contexts and technologies) and those media allow us to extend ourselves (to perceive or to act) in various directions. For example I wear clothes that allow me to go out when otherwise it would be too cold. I use a phone to talk to people who are a long way away. I use an electric light to read when it is dark outside. In all these interactions we can see people as present within a medium—the medium of clothes, of the phone, of light—and, as a result, of being able to engage in experiences that otherwise they wouldn't have. These media also provide opportunities for people as they contain resources that people can use to formulate intentions and to carry them out. For example you might see a sign for museum or art gallery and decide to go and visit it. You might need to buy a parking ticket. You look around, see a ticket machine and read the instructions printed on the machine on how to use it and on the times when you need to. The Pact environments provide informational and interactional resources that significantly impact the overall UX.

In this chapter we explore the characteristics of the media that enable people to have experiences and that impact the ways in which people sense, feel, think and act. This is philosophically an interesting and still controversial area. Ideas on how humans come to know, communicate and think—cognitive psychology—have changed a lot in the last thirty years. The importance of the body and of emotion to thinking and reasoning is now recognized to be much more important than it was.

This chapter is about the C and T of Pact and how they constitute the media within which people can act. But it is also to do with the nature of the P and how the fact that people have bodies affects how they think and feel, and how they come to know. It is about the coupling of people and their environments and the mediating effects that contexts and technologies have on actions.

2.1   UNDERSTANDING MEDIA

Shaleph O'Neil (2008) defines a medium as "the physical elements and attributes of our relationships to the world that allow us to embed our thoughts and ideas in them in order to make them manifest" (p. 10). He explains how a medium is something we use to communicate with, something that sits between people and those they are communicating with. It acts on behalf of people by relaying messages. It is something we put our thoughts, ideas and feelings into. And he emphasizes the physicality of a medium, or the plural, media. A medium has to be physical, otherwise it would not be able to do these things; there would be nothing to make thoughts, ideas and feelings perceptible to others. Being physical the medium also includes our bodies and the movements, gestures, touches, perceptions and audible expressions that we have.

Since media are physical they can be shaped by human endeavor. Malcolm McCullough in his book *Abstracting Craft* discusses the properties that media have that enable people to interact with them to shape them in different ways. For example, wood can be carved with a knife and shaped into all manner of forms, but if it is too thin it will break. Steel requires different tools to shape it, but can be made as thin as wire in which case it has different properties from a rigid steel bar. Different media have different properties, which mean that they can express different things, they can hold different ideas and they offer different ways of interacting with them. Thus it is vital for designers to understand the properties of the materials, or media, that they work with. A photographer needs to understand cameras, lenses, lighting and Photoshop. A jewelry designer needs to understand the properties of different metals and precious stones. An interaction designer needs to know about the different interactive media that there are, about different sensors and actuators, different operating systems and application software.

There is another concept of media that needs addressing, namely the mass media; television, newspapers, communications media, social media and so on. Here discussions usually focus around the impact of media on society and the politics of media and media owners. Couldry and McCarthy (2004) bring together a number of writers and cultural theorists, primarily from a background in geography and spatiality, in their book *MediaSpace*. MediaSpace is a concept that aims to embrace both the spaces created by media forms such as TV and cinema (but also by modern forms such as the mobile phone or "smart house") and the spaces created by media such as virtual reality and computer games. Their analysis of media is where "media and space quite literally merge in architectural infrastructure" (p. 2). Their analysis is primarily focused on the social impact that new media has and on how new media are changing society. "Media forms shape and are shaped by the experience of social space" (p. xx). They describe media as a social process and focus on media production and consumption. Their analysis crosses five levels of mediaspace: studying media representations; studying how media flows across spaces and creates new social spaces; the production and consumption of media; the scale-effects of media, such as the effect that Twitter has had on communications; studying how people experience new media spaces.

So, just as we identified the level of abstraction as an important part of the analysis of interactivity in Chapter 1, so we can see this level of abstraction at work in media spaces. We are embedded in media at different levels of abstraction and we can choose to design, discuss and analyze people's existence in, and interaction with, media at various different levels of abstraction. However, at each level of abstraction we need to be cognizant of O'Neil's argument that a medium is a place for the expression of ideas and feelings that other people can perceive and interact with. Fiona Allan, writing about smart houses in Couldry and McCarthy (2004), defines a medium as the "physical elements and attributes of our relationship to the world that allow us to embed our thoughts and ideas in them in order to make them manifest." Media are made from different materials that affect how the medium can be manipulated and shaped. The author/designer shapes the material and the reader/consumer perceives the shaped material and engages in the social construction of the designers' intentions.

The ideas and feelings that are in a medium constitute the content of that medium. So a medium has both expression (its form) and content. However, if we couple this with the ideas of levels of abstraction, we arrive at an interesting phenomenon. The content of a medium is always another medium. And this medium has a form of expression and some content that in its turn has an expression and some content. Bolter and Grusin (2000) also develop this idea of the content of a medium always being another medium in their book *Remediation*. They distinguish two characteristics of media. Immediacy is when the medium appears to disappear from an interaction and the user of that medium interacts directly with the content. Hypermedia is where the interaction is with the medium itself (the expression rather than the content) and the characteristics of the medium are made to stand out. Bolter develops these ideas with his co-author Gromala in their book *Windows and Mirrors* (Bolter and Gromala, 2003).

Immediacy is the view of a medium as looking through it directly onto the content. A window in a house is a good example of this immediacy, because the medium (the window) disappears from our perception allowing us to perceive what is beyond it. In a similar way a virtual reality headset has two small displays just in front of the user's eyes, allowing the person to concentrate on the content being displayed. The effect of a large screen and darkened room in a cinema also has the effect of focusing the audience's attention on the content of the film rather than on the technical expression that makes the filmic space possible. A live television broadcast of a major event may also produce this effect of immediacy.

Hypermediacy focuses on the expression side of the medium. If the window is dirty then it will interfere with a person's perception of the outside world. If the graphics in a virtual reality headset are not rendered quickly enough the experience will be impoverished and the user will focus on the graphics themselves rather than what they are supposed to represent. A person standing up in front of the cinemagoer can ruin the illusion of the big screen and a breakdown in the outside broadcast set up can break the sense of engagement with the unfolding story.

When confronted with the medium itself, either because of a breakdown, or because of a change in perception by the consumer the levels of abstraction at which the medium is being looked at become clear. Consider the number of people and the technologies involved in the medium that we call "outside broadcast," or that are involved in the medium of cinema or virtual reality. These are highly complex technological feats involving sometimes thousands of people over long periods of time. Embedded within a medium such as cinema are many other media such as acting, lighting, sound, film and so on. Moreover these media build upon previous generations of technologies in terms of both the content and the form, "remediating" as Bolter and Grusin say, the media that have gone before.

In the case of cinema, television broadcasts and virtual reality the contribution of technologies to the creation of a medium is clear to see. At the other end of the spectrum, our shoes are media, my glasses are media, my chair is media and the building and city that I am living in are media. All technologies are media consisting of some content and a form that constrains or affords certain activities and expresses ideas, feelings and thoughts. If we consider shoes as media then we can discuss the shape and color in terms of aesthetics. We can discuss the politics of the brand and the ethics of the company that produced them. We can discuss the activities that the shoes allow me to undertake (e.g., can I run in them?).

So, technologies are media that extend human capabilities in different directions and new technologies offer opportunities for new extensions. Google, for example, has given people a new medium for finding things on the Internet. This new medium changes the way people behave and the way they think. We used to have to classify and organize our information into files and folders so that we could find it again. Now, many people rely on a Google search to find something when they need it. Wikipedia has provided a new medium for collecting encyclopedic knowledge. Encyclopedias used to be authored by individual experts, but now they are authored by multiple people with knowledge and interest in the subject. So, when designers create a new piece of software they introduce another extension opportunity for people. The different social media such as Twitter, Facebook and Instagram enable different forms of expression, different channels of communication and different content to be produced and consumed. These new media change the nature of the interaction between people and the interaction between people and the world.

Returning to the Pact representation of interaction that we introduced in Chapter 1, we can see that we cannot take the person out of the whole experience and this whole is the person in their media. With each technology and their interaction with it people are able to extend themselves to undertake some activities in contexts producing content, inscribing content on the world, and consuming content.

2.2   EMBODIMENT

One of the most important developments in the recent history of cognitive science is the recognition that knowing, thinking and feeling do not happen in the brain. It is embodied in people. Although the importance of embodiment to psychology had been recognized as far back as 1900 within the pragmatist school of philosophy in the U.S., when William James wrote "We think; and as we think we feel our bodily selves as the seat of the thinking." Pragmatism fell out of favor during the rest of the twentieth century. Now it is firmly back on the agenda and notions of embodiment can be found throughout the literature on cognition. Tim Rohrer (2005) provides a thorough treatment.

The idea that thought and language may be based on physically based metaphors and image schemata has been developed by the linguists George Lakoff and Mark Johnson. In 1980, Lakoff and Johnson published their book *Metaphors We Live By* (Lakoff and Johnson, 1980). This groundbreaking book argued that language and thought were based on a limited number of fundamental, conceptual metaphors. They argued that metaphor is central to how humans thought. Many metaphors were not recognized as metaphors because they had been so entrenched into our ways of thinking and talking that we no longer saw them at all. They gave examples such as "knowing is seeing" (e.g., I see what you mean), "up is good" (e.g., he is climbing the ladder of success).

The discovery of the systematic embedding of metaphors was accompanied by another key insight. These metaphors were based on embodied experience. These fundamental, conceptual metaphors derive from the fact that we are people living in the world. For example, we experience boxes, cups and cupboards and indeed our bodies as containers. All of these have a certain structure, namely there is an inside and an outside, and enable certain functions; you can put things in and take things out. Their argument was that these fundamental concepts, based in our experience of living in the world, are the foundation of the ways in which we conceptualize the world; they are the basis of cognition. Another example is a path. A path goes from a source to a destination and hence through all the points in between. This new view of cognition, sometimes known as experientialism, was built on basic concepts and physical actions grounded in spatial experiences and the metaphorical projection from the basic concepts to more abstract thoughts. Their later work continues to explore the ideas further resulting in *The Philosophy of the Flesh* (Lakoff and Johnson, 1999). This book brings together all the philosophy and the physiological evidence to support this view that cognition is derived from the fact that we are embodied people.

Another central aspect of Lakoff and Johnson's theories are image schemas: "embodied patterns of meaningfully organized experience, such as structures of bodily movements and perceptual interactions." Experience is structured in a significant way prior to, and independently of, any concepts. Image schemas are grounded in physical and social experiences and these give the basic logic and concepts to the schema. Other examples of conceptual metaphor include considering anger as containment. "He was boiling over with rage," "steam was coming out of his ears" and so on. These ways of thinking about anger arise from our experience of containment and what happens to liquids in containers when they are heated up.

There is a whole collection of image schemas that have been studied that reflect these embodied experiences. They include part-whole (things are made up from components), center-periphery (central to something or on the edge), link, cycle, iteration, contact, adjacency, pushing, pulling, propelling, support, balance, straight-curved, near-far, front-back, above-below. Image schemas have a logic to them and it is this logic that is preserved when we apply the metaphor from a more embodied concept to a more abstract concept. Abstract thought comes about by projecting the structure and functions of a physically grounded image schema through metaphor onto a more abstract domain. Image schemas have been employed in interaction design (e.g., Hurtienne et al., 2008) as a good way of helping people to understand features of interactive experiences as we discuss in Chapter 6.

Embodiment is also apparent at a socio-cultural level. The first manifestation of this is the recognition that when people think, they make use of resources that are in the external world. A simple example that is often given here is the use of a shopping list. Rather than keeping everything in your head, when you go shopping, it makes sense to offload some of the cognitive effort of remembering to things that are in the environment. A shopping list is a good example. In activities such as traveling, people would always make use of signposts in the environment to guide them to their destination. (However, reflect on how this has changed with the invention of Tom Tom satnav systems).

The second piece of evidence here is that the stuff that is in the world affects how we think. John Haugeland (1995) talks about how the road to San Jose is a fundamental part of how we think about getting to San Jose and Andy Clark (2008) gives many other examples. Indeed Clark takes this argument much further in arguing for the "extended mind" theory of cognition and gives an example of one person who uses a notebook to record the address of a museum he wants to visit and one person who keeps this knowledge in her head. Clark argues that the cognition involved is essentially the same. So long as an external entity is "readily available," "trustworthy" and "easily accessible" it can be included as part of a cognitive system (Clark and Chalmers, 1998).

Related ideas can be found in Maurice Merleau-Ponty's philosophy (from the 1960s) about how we pick up information from the world (Merleau-Ponty, 1962) and J. J. Gibson's ideas about how the world provides affordances for people where affordances are the relationships between the properties of the world and the perceptions of people (Gibson, 1979). The fact that people have bodies is essential for understanding how perception and cognition function. The relationships between people and their environment are fundamental for recognizing opportunities and constraints on action.

Ed Hutchins undertook a number of famous studies of navigation in Polynesia in his book *Cognition in the Wild* (Hutchins, 1996) that illustrate how socio-cultural embodiment affects cognition and perception of the relationships between Polynesian islands. Western navigators might use an astrolabe, which is a device that physically presents navigational knowledge of the spatial relationships between celestial bodies as a set of rotating discs. The interaction here is a physical manipulation of these discs and the astrolabe represents externalized cognition. In contrast the Polynesian navigators relied on sea currents, the presence of birds and an oral culture to help with navigation. Cognition is still externalized, or distributed, but through very different media.

2.2.1 PHENOMENOLOGY AND EMBODIMENT

Phenomenology is a philosophical position that distances itself from looking for an objective reality and instead focuses on the everyday experiences of people and the phenomena that they encounter. The development of phenomenology is generally credited to the German philosopher Edmund Husserl (1859–1938). It was developed through one of his students Martin Heidegger (1889–1976) and adopted and developed by other important twentieth-century philosophers including Maurice Merleau-Ponty (1908–1961). Drawing on this phenomenological philosophy Paul Dourish introduced ideas of embodied cognition to the HCI and interaction design community in his book *Where the Action Is* (Dourish, 2004). For Dourish, phenomenology is about the tight coupling of action and meaning. Actions take on meaning for people. Coupling is concerned with making the relationship between actions and meaning effective. If objects and relationships are coupled then effects of actions can be passed through the system. Dourish uses the familiar example of a hammer (also used by Heidegger) to illustrate coupling. When you use a hammer it becomes an extension to your arm (it is coupled) and you act through the hammer onto the nail. You are engaged in the activity of hammering.

From this theory of embodied interaction Dourish goes on to develop some high-level design principles concerning computation as a medium and how people through embodied interaction turn action into meaning. Embodiment is "phenomenological presence" and embodied interaction is "the creation, manipulation and sharing of meaning through engaged interaction with artifacts."

The pragmatist philosophy was based in experience of the everyday world, distancing itself from the other philosophy of its day that looked at a disembodied "logical" view of the world. Pragmatism resonates with phenomenological views of experience. These deny that it is appropriate to analyze whole experiences in terms of their parts and recognize the whole of some phenomenon needs to be understood if the essence of that phenomenon is to be uncovered. McCarthy and Wright pursue this holistic view in *Technology as Experience* (2004), drawing on the work of another pragmatist, John Dewey. They also emphasize the "felt sense" of experience. Both James and Dewey built on the work of the person credited by James as the founder of this philosophical movement, Charles Sanders Peirce (1839–1914). Peirce also developed a form of phenomenology at the same time as Husserl, but as far as we know they were unaware of each other's work (Spiegelberg, 1956). Peirce was also a founder of the next thing we consider, semiotics.

2.3   SEMIOTICS

Embodiment is a view of people living in the world that recognizes that the way we think is influenced by the fact that we have bodies and live in a physical and cultural world. In its turn the physical structures in the world influence the way we think and hold our thoughts, ideas and emotions. For example, we have seen how the road to San Jose influences the cognitive processes of working out how to get to San Jose. We have also seen how Polynesian navigators make use of sea currents and bird movements to navigate whereas Western navigators make use of astrolabes. And of course modern-day car drivers make use of satellite navigation ("Tom Tom" or satnav) systems. So, how should we describe this environment in which all these things are embedded?

The answer is to look at semiotics because semiotics concerns the use people make of signs. Clearly the Polynesian navigators are using signs of birds and currents to navigate. The Western navigators are making use of the markings on the discs of the astrolabe and the interaction with the device to navigate. The car drivers listen to the instructions given by the satnav and look at the signs on the screen and alongside the road.

As with interaction and media, semiotics can be applied at many different levels of abstraction. It can be used by philosophers trying to understand how meanings are created, and understood. It is used by cultural commentators discussing the significance of images, texts or events. It is used by politicians, advertisers and others trying to persuade people to adopt a certain understanding toward some product or idea. Semiotics is about how people know, communicate and reason about the world that focuses not on how the brain works, but on the interaction between the media objects in the world and our ideas and feelings.

For example, Christian Metz (1974) looks at the relationship between codes that exist in cinema and films, how specific "shots" are used and how cultural codes allow people to derive meaning. Kress and van Leeuwen (1996) look at the semiotics of visual images. Jacques Bertin (1981) looks at the semiotics of graphics providing a sound theoretical grounding for the presentation of information that has been extended by Stuart Card (2012) to the realm of computer displays and interactive visualizations. Semiotic principles extend out from information design such as this to maps, signage and wayfinding support (Arthur and Passini, 2002). In HCI de Souza has developed a method for user interface design based on semiotics (de Souza, 2005) and Shaleph O'Neil applies semiotics to interactive media (O'Neil, 2008).

The basic idea underlying semiotics is that some of the things in the world can be used to help us think and communicate with others. Our views of semiotics originate once again at the turn of the twentieth century. In Europe semiotic ideas were being developed by Ferdinand de Saussure (in 1916, see de Saussure, 2013) and in America through the philosophy of Charles Sanders Peirce. Underpinned by his own study of phenomenological experience, Peirce established the basis of his semiotics.

Building on Peirce and Saussure, Umberto Eco (1976) provides a definition of signs and se-miotics that takes into account the myriad social, cultural and contextual issues that underlie every instance of sign use. In doing so Eco proposes a theory of semiotics in terms of the use of signs as acts of coding and decoding messages with reference to sets of culturally defined conventions. The socio-cultural aspects of semiotics and the importance of context in evaluating meaning are central to his theory.

The basic semiotic concept consists of a signifier (or expression) and a signified (or content), the two always going together to act as a sign, or "sign-vehicle." Just as we saw at the beginning of this chapter how the content of a medium is always another medium, so both the expression and content of signs have a substance and a form that can be studied as semiotics in their own right. For example, a red light might be a sign for "danger." The light has an expression—red or not—which comes from the substance of the electricity flowing through the lamp. On the other side of the coin the form of the content is danger, but the substance will be realized according to different contexts and circumstances. For example, if this situation were encountered by a train driver at a station, the danger signified by the red light might have the meaningful substance of another train on the track. If a red light is encountered on a TV set it probably signifies that the TV set is turned off.

Another key concept in semiotics is the level of abstraction that is adopted by people with different interests. If we return to the case of the red light signifying danger, physicists, for exam-ple, might be interested in the physical characteristics of the light and amount of electrical power needed to light a lamp. For them photons might be the signals and optics might be the continuum. For cultural commentators red lights are the signals, "danger," "stop," traffic lights and other cultural artifacts are the meanings of interest and such things as their position in society and their impact on individual identity or gender stereotyping constitute the continuum of the signs.

Eco, in his many writings, goes on to develop a rich theory of the different types of signs and the different types of content that they express. There is also an important difference between taking a sign to mean something—to denote a particular object, say—and to consider the various other ideas—the connotations—that arise from this relationship. At a further level of abstraction, critics may use these connotations to make rich, meta-level inferences from media. The great exponent of this was Roland Barthes who used semiotics to comment on the culture, feelings and stories revealed by everyday images such as a shopping bag or advertising poster.

In interaction design the use of semiotics in this has been advocated in terms of interaction criticism (Bardzell, 2011). "By *interaction criticism* we mean rigorous interpretive analysis that ex-plicates how elements of the interface, through their relationships to each other, produce certain meanings, affects, moods, and intuitions in the people that interact with them." They map out the relationships between computer artifacts and culture and explore how various different forms of critical theory can inform interaction design.

2.4   BEING IN THE WORLD

If we reflect on these ideas of media, embodiment and semiotics, we can arrive at a description of people interacting in the world that is useful for looking at interaction design and user experience. The human condition arises from being in an enormously rich, dynamic, multi-faceted environment in which people are interpreting things, forming intentions, undertaking actions, making things and creating objects, feeling sensations, feeling emotions, having ideas, chewing over possible scenarios, creating content and inscribing signs on the physical fabric of the world.

As babies we interact with a physical and cultural world and hence develop neurological structures, concepts and categories that are formed or informed by these physical and cultural experiences. These are the basic categories and image schemata that form the basis of higher-level functions as we employ metaphorical projections to new experiences. So we can understand anger in terms of steam, or success in terms of going up.

But of course this physical and cultural world is full of objects and signs that other people have left there. All the videos on YouTube and music on iTunes, the photos of Flickr and the texts on Tumblr and all the emails, tweets, texts and phone conversations that happen every day are part of this environment. This is the medium in which people must exist, the media space, along with all the physical and social aspects of being-in-the-world. This brings us to some important conceptions of how we see people as being in the world.

Tim Ingold argues that we must not see the world as surrounding people, but rather as people moving through paths through rich cultural contexts (Ingold, 2009). He develops these ideas of openness and enclosure by opposing the notion that people are dwelling in a space (as Heidegger would have it) with the notion that people inhabit a world with the earth below and the sky above and therefore a horizon of perception that moves as people move. People are not in a simple enclosure in their world. He says, "It is at this surface—conceived as an interface not just between the solid substance of the earth and its gaseous atmosphere but between matter and mind, and between sensation and cognition—that all knowledge is constituted" (Ingold, 2000, pp. 212–214). Ingold goes on to question why so few philosophers, such as Gibson and Heidegger, discuss the weather in their reasoning about places. They see places as being in a room or being in a clearing in a forest. Ingold, on the other hand sees living as being in a weather-world where the weather binds the sky and earth together. People are immersed in the medium of the flux and flow of the weather. As we have seen above, we see people as being in the medium of all objects and semiotics that make up the cultural context.

Ed Hutchins pursues a similar argument, arguing that thinking lies in the interactions of brain and body with the world. Interactions are not the result of some underlying thought processes applied to the world. They are the thinking processes themselves (Hutchins, 2010). These ideas are picked up by another area of the study of the human condition, namely archaeology. Lambros Malafouris in his book *How Things Shape the Mind* (Malafouris, 2013) brings these ideas to archaeology, criticizing much traditional archaeology, and develops material engagement theory that focuses on the process of human development rather than the when and where of human development. Thus the focus is on understanding the co-evolution of brains, bodies and things. He argues that whereas traditional archaeology would see the stone-age man as having an intention to shape an axe out of a flint and then to consciously work away at it, the alternative view is to see that most of the thinking takes place where the hand meets the stone; in the interaction of people with their environment.

This issue of deciding where we place boundaries in the analysis of people in the world is critical. Malafouris uses the famous example of the blind man's stick to illustrate both the difficulty of drawing boundaries and the argument for embodied and embedded cognition. Where does the blind man's self end and the world begin? Our answer to this is that the stick is yet another medium that the blind man is engaged in. In a similar way Malafouris goes on to develop his material engagement theory in terms of mediation, the temporal nature of being human and the plastic effects that objects and interactions have on how people think.

2.4.1   PRESENCE

As a final contribution to the debate about how people perceive and act in the world we can look at the philosophy of telepresence. The term "telepresence" was coined in the 1980s in order to describe the sense of and transportation to another place that can be felt with immersive virtual reality systems. It soon became conflated with the philosophical idea of "presence" as the sense of knowing where you are and knowing that you are. Since then the concept has been widely discussed and a number of different views have been developed. In the mid 1990s, coming from the U.S. military perspective, Witmer and Singer (1998) proposed that presence was "being there" and developed a questionnaire to measure the sense of presence. Coming from a media and communication perspective, Lombard and Ditton (1997) proposed a definition that presence was "the perceptual illusion of non-mediation." In their comprehensive review of issues of presence they argue that the sense of presence comes about when people do not notice the medium through which they are interacting with some content. More recently, however, the philosopher Luciano Floridi has questioned this definition, arguing that presence should not be defined in negative terms. He proposes that presence is the successful observation of entities in our surroundings (Floridi, 2007).

Coming from a psychological and philosophical position Riva et al. (2004) argue that there is an essential evolutionary need for a sense of presence. Presence is the result of an evolved neuropsychological process that allows people to differentiate between the self and the other (the environment). Presence is attention to the non-self, the external world that is needed for survival in addition to emotional appraisal of events. In short, people need to know what is real and what is not if they are to survive. People usually interact with their environment through some technologies, even if those technologies are shoes and shirts, spectacles and hammers. When technologies are perceived as part of self, people will feel a strong presence in them. They argue that when the technology that mediates the interactions with the environment appears to disappear—feels part of the self—there is no effort of action or effort of access to information in the environment. In Heidegger's terms things are ready-to-hand. Thus technology allows people to extend themselves. Clearly this has resonances with material engagement theory and with the example of the blind man's stick used by Malafouris (2013).

Ijsselsteijn and Riva (2003) focus on presence as distal attribution, on the interplay between internal presence (personal presence) and external presence enabled by technologies (telepresence). A key feature of presence is the ability to interact and modify the environment, not simply observe it. Riva argues that presence is the "intuitive successful action in the environment." Floridi says something similar while also emphasizing that we need to consider the level of abstraction when making judgments about presence. The emphasis on action is important as it brings with it the concepts of volition and intention into a discussion of presence. People want to bring about some change in the environment, to enact some change. In Riva et al. (2011) they bring these arguments together arguing that presence is the missing link between cognition and volition. Presence locates itself in an external and cultural space and can act in it. Presence provides feedback to the self about the status of its activity and "tunes" its activity so that it is intuitive, or non-mediated.

Presence, then, is interacting directly with the content of media. But it would be wrong to see this as a single thing. As we have seen interactions are multi-layered, built upon one another, and there are many mediums (media) through which we are acting at any one time. As soon as I have accessed a medium's content and incorporated this, my new extended self can interact at the next level of abstraction in that medium. However, I might then access and incorporate some other medium's content thus extending myself in another direction. This may happen physically such as when I move to feel present in a particular place, or it may happen conceptually such as when I have a conversation with another person.

This view of presence as interaction with the content of media shares ideas with many recent and older accounts. Views of presence that foreground being able to act in the environment which suggest physical action, are replaced by the ability to add, change and manipulate content. Whereas accounts of presence tend to look at the environment of the self as a single technologically mediated entity, our view recognizes the multi-layered and multi-faceted view of presence. Thus presence does not require sophisticated computing equipment. At its most basic, the blind person's stick is an example of a technology, or a medium, that allows the person to reach out and be present of a more distant world. Telepresence allows us to reach beyond the confines of our body. Of course if we do have sophisticated computing technologies, then we can be present on Mars, controlling a remote vehicle, or as a surgeon feeling present when undertaking a remote operation. All manner of simple media such as eye-glasses, hearing aids and so on extend our natural presence away from the confines of the body. New media make us present of certain attributes of the world and allow us to be present of things that our five senses would not allow us to be present of.

Merleau-Ponty (1962) distinguished the objective body from the phenomenological body and it is this person-in-media that corresponds to the phenomenological self that helps to explain how we can feel present in digital environments such as virtual worlds. Furthermore, to be present is to be in a place. Place is the medium in which we make ourselves as has been recognized by many writers such as Merleau-Ponty and Heidegger (1927 see Heidegger, 2010).

One important aspect of presence that relates very much to the idea of medium and tools providing extensions to people is the idea of incorporation. In a discussion of peripersonal spaces, Lenti and Decortis (2010) distinguish between people having extensions and people incorporating objects and knowledge into their (phenomenal) body. Prostheses are extensions to the body that have been incorporated (perhaps only temporarily). These can be opposed with extensions that are not incorporated. When we use tools our physical body is extended and the action space is enlarged. Thus the blind man's stick is incorporated into his body and extends his presence. Heidegger's hammer that is ready-to-hand when in use by the practiced carpenter is another example of a prosthetic. In these circumstances the extensions become a knowing part of the body and part of one's body model and there is a feeling of ownership.

There are fascinating experiments with monkeys using a rake to get food demonstrating how the rake becomes an extension of the monkey. Other experiments deal with the "phantom hand" where a rubber hand is placed next to a person's real hand, which is then covered over. When the rubber hand is stroked the person feels their real hand being stroked. There are of course many stories of amputees being able to feel their amputated limb. Thus we can see the sense of presence as being extended with tools and other media further into the different media of interaction.

2.5 SUMMARY

So we have now explored the Pact elements a bit further and can understand that contexts and technologies create the medium within which people can act. There is an essential physicality to these media that derives from the fact that humans are embodied. The concepts that we develop, how we classify things and how we approach interaction derive from the embodied and embedded notion of interaction. For interaction designers, this means that they need to design "at a human scale." Designers should not be too abstract, nor too technologically focused, but instead design with an understanding of the essential nature of Pact.

We recognize that people are always embedded in a number of media. These media are fundamental to the human ability to think, communicate and interact with others, because the media holds ideas and concepts for people. A medium must exist in order to make ideas physical so that people can interact with others, whether the medium is words, objects or interfaces. The stuff of the world, including our bodies, has the capacity to be formed and reformed by physical manipulation, in order to represent ideas. In doing so, the stuff of the world holds concepts for us, relieving us of the need to keep them in our heads. This allows us to perceive them, recognize them and reuse them as and when we need. The stuff of the world is able to act as a medium through which we can communicate and interact because it is malleable and responsive to physical transformation. In addition people are physical beings that can act on it taking advantage of the physical laws of cause and effect. This allows people to "off-load" cognition into the environment and mark the world around them, creating content in the medium, giving form to thoughts and experiences.

CHAPTER 3

Physical Space

Despite the fact that much interaction design is concerned with the development of mobile apps and websites, the physical environment is increasingly important to spaces of interaction and to UX. Locative media are interactive systems designed to take advantage of a person's physical location either outside using the global positioning system (GPS) or inside using beacons. In these situations understanding the physical space in which interaction takes place is central to providing a good UX. The design of responsive environments is another area where designers need to think about physical and technological spaces and with the coming Internet of Things, interaction design will be increasingly distributed across physical space.

There are many, many perspectives on the concept of physical space ranging from discussions in Computer Supported Cooperative Working (CSCW) and Human-Computer Interaction (HCI) literature, to presence research, to architecture, to urban studies, to cultural geography, to semiotics, to sociology, to anthropology, to environmental studies, to psychology, to art, to general philosophy. Each of these disciplines highlights different aspects of the concept, often at very different scales, from cities, to communities, to the design of offices and individual or collaborative experiences. Finding one's way through this literature is difficult and is compounded by the inescapable fact that writers tend to explore the concept within their own cultural and historical setting.

Our focus is on places in the context of interaction design. There is a wealth of material on the subject of space and place studies that can be explored and so inevitably we can only hope to surf the main areas that contribute to interaction and experience design. The aim of this chapter, then, is to explore the concepts of physical spaces relevant to interaction design and to point to interesting diversions for those who want to go further into the philosophy and culture of space and place.

3.1   SPACE AND PLACE

In the world of CSCW spaces and places of interaction have been discussed since the mid-1990s. Harrison and Dourish (1996) presented an early distinction between space and place that was revisited by Dourish 10 years later (2006). In the early paper they explored the difference between space and place based broadly on a distinction between space as the notion of geometry and geography and place as "space + meaning." In Dourish's later paper he moves away from this overly simple distinction and recognizes both space and place to be complex and subjective constructs. Dourish draws on a number of accounts of cultural geography to look at the social construction of space and on the relationships between technology, mediated practice and spaces of interaction. He highlights the nature of the modern world with the multiple interrelated spatial systems and infrastructures and how these open up new ways of working and how people come to understand spaces through the practices of space. Drawing on Michel de Certeau's work (1984) he distinguishes strategic practices of space (characterized by design) and tactical practices of space. The tactical practices of space are concerned with how the space is used; the production of spaces through use. This idea of the production of space is also developed by Henri Lefebrve, a Marxist sociologist writing in the 1970s (Lefebvre, 1991).

So, designers and architects may be responsible for the overall form of a space, but it is the people interacting with and within that space that produces the sense of place and being. Building on this work, Lentini and Decoris identify five types of experience of place; the geometric and geographic, the sensorial, the cultural, the personal and the relational (Lentini and Decortis, 2010).

Heidegger is frequently cited in discussions about space and place, focusing on his ideas of being and of dwelling. Heidegger used the word *Dasein* to denote his concept of being-in-the-world. People are always in a place and it does not make sense to talk about people without talking about the places and what they are doing there. However, many of Heidegger's examples are very pastoral and nostalgic and do not extend easily to places that mix digital and physical experiences. For example he will use examples of how the river Ruhr was ruined by the development of power stations or he will talk about the characteristics of places where there is a bridge over a small stream. Heidegger's contribution to the philosophy of place and technology is ambivalent in that he seems to favor older technologies over the modern, but at the same time recognizes that technologies bring forth and reveal the sense of being.

Jeff Malpas provides a rich and in-depth understanding of the philosophy of place and of Heidegger's philosophy in his book *Place and Experience* (Malpas, 1999). He makes the argument that the very identities of people are bound up with notions of place and more, "a central theme in the conceptual explorations undertaken in the following pages [of his book] is that the very possibility of the appearance of things—of objects, or self, and of others—is possible only within the all embracing compass of place" (pp. 14–15). For Malpas, place requires bodies and movement (cf. ideas of embodiment in Chapter 2). Place is "space as it presents itself" and any thinking creature requires a "grasp of space" conceptually or behaviorally. This grasp of space depends on a creature's sensory, cognitive and motor abilities and the creature's capacity of movement and activity. He goes on to explore the difference between a rat moving through a maze, where there is a clear behavioral grasp of space and a human who has behavioral grasp and a conceptual grasp of space. Moreover the human has an egocentric grasp of space in distinguishing the self from the environment and an allocentric grasp of space (otherwise called a cognitive map) that understands that the map is a representation. In other words people understand the semiotic level of description. Thus place is seen as a structure within which experiences are possible.

Heidegger was a phenomenologist who focused on the experience of being. Other phenomenological treatments of spaces and places are found in the works of Li-Fu Tuan (1977) and Edward Relph (1976), both writing in the 1970s. Relph distinguishes between space and place by saying "when space feels thoroughly familiar to us it has become place" (p. 73) and Tuan that "it transforms places as it acquires definition and meaning." Relph's monograph takes an explicitly phenomenological and holistic stance toward appreciating places. He defines three components of "place identity," the physical setting, the activities afforded by the place and the meanings and affect attributed to the place.

Gustafson's (2001) conceptualization of place draws on empirical work in the form of an interview survey to identify three poles that can be used to understand places. Self concerns the individual's life-path, emotions, activities and identification. Environment concerns the physical environment, distinctive features and events, the type of place and its localization. The characteristics of other people in the place characterize the third pole. Jorgensen and Stedman (2001) developed their view of place based on interviews with Swedish second home owners, again highlighted issues of self, the activities and the emotional attitudes toward place. Turner and Turner (2006) take these characteristics of place and use them to look at people's reactions to photorealistic virtual reality representations of real places, concluding that a framework based around the physical, the activities, the affect and the social interactions is an effective way of understanding places.

We used a similar structure when we developed a "place probe." Our aim was to understand the characteristics of place that people find important, for the purpose of creating photorealistic representations of places (Benyon, et al., 2005). The probe consisted of a number of items—a semantic differential of adjectives describing spaces, draw a picture of the space, provide three words that capture the essence of the space—that aimed to elicit people's conceptualization of different spaces in a phenomenological way.

Overall, then, the message is that spaces and places need to be seen in a phenomenological way; as a whole rather than as the components that go to make them. In common parlance we move between the words space and place quite happily, referring to a "nice space" or a "nice place," a "large space" or a "large place." What is important is that designers think about the physical characteristics of a place, the activities that people can and do undertake in the place, the feelings and emotions that they have and the personal and social relationships that happen in the place. Most importantly, of course, is that different people will experience places in very different ways at different times. The interaction between people who populate a space, and the objects in a space can result in a variety of interpretations of that place. Examples such as the sense of place experienced by skate-boarders in a city park compared with the sense of place experienced by shoppers or office workers are often cited, or the different feelings that one gets from a place on a sunny day against a dark winter's night.

3.2   ARCHITECTURE

In architecture, another phenomenologist who developed Heidegger's ideas is Christian Nor-berg-Schultz again writing in the 1970s and 80s. He provides a structural view of place in terms of landscape, settlement, space and character (Norberg-Schulz, 1980). He discusses Kevin Lynch's conceptualization of the city in terms of landmarks, nodes, edges and districts (Lynch 1960). Nor-berg-Schulz goes on to explore other spatial concepts such as enclosure, extension, figure-ground, boundary, centralization and proximity. He offers a nice quotation from Heidegger: "the boundary is that from which something begins its presencing" (p. 13). He goes on to discuss character in detail and how architecture makes a site a place, though he emphasizes the structure of a place is not fixed but changes with time. However it is the "Genius Loci" (the spirit of a place) that does not get lost.

Another architect, Gordon Cullen, explains his Townscape Theory in terms of the concept of optics (serial vision), place and content (Cullen, 1964). Optics concerns the unfolding experience of walking through a space. The concept of place is concerned with one's emotional reaction to the position of their body in its environment. Cullen states that "the human being is constantly aware of his position in the environment, […] he feels the need for a sense of place and […] this sense of identity is coupled with an awareness of elsewhere" (p.12). Content is defined by the fabric of towns: color, texture, scale, style, character, personality and uniqueness. These fabrics are used to create the individual elements of the urban space and "to create symmetry, balance, perfection, and conformity" (p. 11).

David Canter (1977) takes a more psychological view and describes a faceted theory of place that aims to integrate an environmental psychology perspective with one coming from architecture. He argues that form, function, and space are the key features most associated with people's experiences of buildings and other spaces. They combine the individual, social and cultural perspectives. His theory of place is a theory of situated activities. Pulling these ideas together he identifies four key facets—function, objectives, scale of interaction and aspects of design—to develop a rich view of places. The function facet considers the centrality of certain functions to certain parts of the overall place. The objectives focus on the individual, social or cultural perspective being taken. The scale of the place refers to the environmental scale and whether one is considering immediate, local or distant relationships and the design facet considers the form, function and spatial relations of a place. The interaction of these facets produces different typologies of places.

Canter uses his theory to look at the work of Christopher Alexander (1979) who sought to capture the experience of spaces as a set of over 250 architectural patterns. Each pattern describes a solution to a classic design problem, or design situation. The patterns are heavily biased to a particular view of being (the timeless way of building) capturing what Alexander believed to be good design solutions. Benyon et al. (2005) try to get a rich description of people's experiences of places by looking at activity patterns, physical patterns and patterns of meaning and affect. As with Alexandrian patterns, the patterns make use of other patterns in a network structure referring to other patterns to create a pattern language for design of spaces.

In museum design, space syntax (Hillier and Hansen, 1984) has been used to explore design options with the aim of optimizing the complex relationships between the curated objects, the gallery spaces, the museum as a whole, the movement through the museum and the presence and experiences of people in that space. Spatial interactivity is seen as important as technological interactivity. Indeed space syntax is a very general way of looking at spaces that focuses on the key features of spatial integration, choice and depth. The approach is to strip away the different types of room, or building, and instead focus on the structure in terms of how closely integrated the different spaces are and how deep the structure is in terms of its connectivity. Looking at where people need to make choices if moving through the space is another tool in the analysis.

3.3   PATTERNS OF PLACE

In architecture Christopher Alexander (1979) has been very influential in introducing the idea of architectural patterns. These are regular good design ideas. For example, it is a good idea to have small parking lots in a neighborhood because very large parking lots are ugly and disrupt the neighborhood. It is a good idea to have pavement cafés in a city where people can sit outside because it creates a nice atmosphere. It is a good idea to have a low wall next to an open area so people can sit on it.

Alexander's patterns for architectural features are at different levels of abstraction—from patterns for walls to patterns for whole cities. Each pattern expresses a relation between a certain context, a certain system of "forces" that occurs repeatedly in that context (i.e., a particular problem, or particular design constraints) and a solution which allows these forces to resolve themselves. Patterns, therefore, refer to other patterns and are part of larger patterns. For example, the pattern "Gallery Surround" proposes that people should be able to walk through a connecting zone such as a balcony to feel connected to the outside world. The "Opening to the Street" pattern says that people on a sidewalk should feel connected to functions inside a building, made possible by direct openings.

Patterns are embodied as concrete prototypes rather than abstract principles and tend to focus on the interactions between the physical form of the built environment and the way in which that inhibits or facilitates various sorts of behavior within it. Pattern languages are not value neutral but instead manifest particular values in their names and more explicitly in their rationales.

Alexander specified over 250 patterns in his book. The pattern descriptions are rich in narrative detail, sometimes include pictures and often refer to other patterns. For example, Pattern 88 "Street Café" is described as follows (with referenced patterns in brackets): neighborhoods are defined by Identifiable Neighborhood (14); their natural points of focus are given by Activity Nodes (30) and Small Public Squares (61). This pattern, and the ones which follow it, give the neighborhood and its points of focus, their identity. The street café provides a unique setting, special to cities: a place where people can sit lazily, legitimately, be on view, and watch the world go by.

Malcolm McCullough (2005) also looks at patterns of place in defining a typology of thirty situated interactions that focus on places and the activities that people undertake there. He divides places, or situations, into workplace, dwelling place, places for conviviality and "on the road." Work places include places for thinking, places for presenting, places for working in groups, places for negotiating, officiating, crafting, associating, learning, cultivating and watching. At home he identifies places for sheltering, recharging, idling, confining, servicing and metering. On the town there are places for socializing, gathering, cruising, belonging, shopping, sporting, attending and commemorating. On the road he identifies places for touring, hoteling, adventuring, driving and walking.

He then goes on to elaborate the characteristics of each of these spaces in terms of the technologies that can be used in the places and the impact that these technologies are having on the activities that people undertake and experiences that people have. This is something we return to in Chapters 7 and 9.

3.4   SPATIAL INTERACTION

Bill Buxton (2009) points out that people have a great spatial literacy and that they are very good at understanding relationships through looking at spatial relationships. For example in a lecture room you will know who is the professor and who are the students because the professor will be at the front of the room. You can recognize two lovers in the park through their spatial interaction. He goes on to look at the different configurations of people and work in his office—from a person popping their head round the door, to working closely with a student on a specific task, to sitting back and chatting. The different conventions for different social settings are reflected in the spatial interactions.

We return to the social space of interaction in Chapter 7. Suffice to say at the moment that people have their own personal space within which they do not like others intruding. This varies greatly across cultures with some cultures hugging and kissing each other while others prefer to maintain more of a distance. The study of personal spaces and relationships is known as proxemics (Hall, 1969).

Going beyond the personal space we can see a variety of different types of interaction that are possible. These go from conversations, to shouting to each other across a room, to using microphones and speakers as extensions to facilitate interaction in a large room or outdoors, to waving at somebody across the street to observing some on the top of a faraway hill.

Besides the spatial constraints and affordances of interaction between people, there are interactions between people and the space itself. Think of the difference between being in a very confined space and being in the open air. There is an important notion of the ambient space, the background for our interactions. Malcolm McCullough calls this the "ambient commons" (Mc-

Cullough, 2013) and with the increasing embedding of sensors and actuators into the environment, the ambient space is becoming increasingly functional. While ambient interaction is usually at the scale of rooms, environmental interaction at a grander scale is increasing.

Another important feature of spatial interaction is that it is nested. Spaces are contained inside other spaces and can be described at different levels of abstraction. We have seen that spaces are perceived differently by different individuals and groups at different times. Different people will appropriate spaces for their own types of activity. At different levels of abstraction people will perceive objects in the spaces, and spaces around the objects.

Objects and spaces can be described by their topological relationships. Topology concerns the relationships between objects in a space and from this to describe distance and direction. However, once again we need to distinguish the level of description from rooms and buildings to neighborhoods to cities, countries and the planet itself. Between the spaces there are liminal regions and seams where spaces come together. These can create niches where certain environmental conditions pertain.

Finally spatial interaction is concerned with movement both at the bodily level through walking, running or dancing and at the environmental level of navigation through the space. Navigation is central to spatial interaction and we return to this in Chapter 8.

3.5   SUMMARY

This brief exploration of space and place is intended to excite and tempt as much as it is to explain. Interested readers are directed first of all to Ed Casey's *Getting Back in Place* (second edition, 2009) where the rich historical, poetic and cultural issues of places, being in places and moving through places are explored in detail. We might spend time discussing *terroir*, the unique sense of place that gives natural products such as wine their unique characteristics. We can explore notions of "here" and "there" in different settings and in different languages and cultures. The Spanish words *este* and *esta* never fail to confuse me as my concept of "this one" and "that one" seems very different from my Spanish shopkeepers! We might consider place from the local inhabitant's perspective or from those who are just passing through and approach the place with the "tourist's gaze" (Urry, 2013). We might consider those soulless impersonal hotels and other examples of non-place. We can focus on the center of spaces or the periphery, the functions that places afford or the emotions that places evoke.

Looking back over these various accounts we finish up with a description of physical space that focuses its structure, the dynamics of the space and the people in the space. In terms of its structure we recognize that there are various objects in the space that are spatially related to each other. At the scale of cities these would be the Lynchian concepts of nodes, edges, landmarks and districts; at the scale of houses these would be rooms. Adding in the form and function of the place gives an analysis of patterns of designing for particular purposes, and for particular emotional or socio-cultural experience.

Describing the relationships between the component spaces leads us to look at the topology of the space, how local or distant the objects are from one another and the direction that they lie in. Thus in addition to the objects in the space (the ontology) and the topology, we need to consider the dynamics of the space, since spaces change over time and objects move (volatility) and the people in the space along with their cultural and social setting, the meanings they make and the activities they undertake (agency).

Increasingly interaction designers are augmenting physical spaces with technologies; the digital space that we consider in the next chapter. The Internet of Things brings further opportunities to augment physical spaces. And of course interaction designers are frequently designing for home, work, social and on-the-move situations.

CHAPTER 4

Digital Space

The digital space is the world of virtual reality, databases, spreadsheets, the internet, music, electronic books, films and videos, Facebook, Twitter, phone calls, Skype and all things digital. It is the same as the popular term "cyberspace," but by foregrounding the digital we highlight other issues. Digital space concerns digital technologies and how people interact with them and through them. It is about communication with other people. It is about how digital devices communicate and interact and about the digital infrastructures that facilitate that. As we know it is thoroughly pervasive and becoming more so. Often the development of some new technology, or new digital spaces, is very disruptive to current practice and can cause major changes in business models and employment as we have seen, for example, in the music industry.

Digital space is the space of bits rather than atoms. It is the intangible but infinitely transmittable and transformable. The digital space concerns data and how it is structured and stored. It concerns the content that is available and the software that is available to manipulate content.

There are many different views on digital spaces and many different people who are interested in digital space from different perspectives. Database people look to how digital data can be organized and structured to represent some domain or "universe of discourse." People who are interested in virtual reality look at the digital space quite differently, focusing on motion, navigation and the representation of people as avatars. Software engineers focus on the objects, methods and delivering functionality.

4.1 DIGITAL TECHNOLOGIES

There are, of course, thousands of different types of digital technologies that are in use nowadays. Finding a sensible and useful way of summing up what they are and what their characteristics are is something of a challenge. The technology magazines and websites usually focus on the speed of processing or the amount of storage that a device has, whether that storage is for processing or whether it is for keeping digital media files. The technology websites such as Techcrunch are the best place to start if you want to find out about technologies. The characteristics of a digital technology will have a big effect on what a person can do with it, the overall UX of using it, what media it can process and what it can connect to.

Digital technologies need content and functions for manipulating that content and they need some media for interacting with people and with other technologies. Some of this content is put into the technology when it is manufactured through pre-programmed microchips. For example some technologies have clock content (time, dates, days and years) and functions built in, others have mathematical functions such as addition and multiplication built in. So my digital clock can check which day a particular date is, but it cannot add up a set of numbers. My digital calculator can add, subtract, multiply and divide, but it cannot tell me the time. Apps will have content relevant to the app built in. For example a weight-watching app will have the calorific value of different foods in it.

In addition to the content that is built in to a technology, technologies usually have some methods, some media, for allowing a user to input data, allowing a user to perceive any output data and ways to communicate data with other technologies. Some technologies have keyboards to allow the input of textual data. Others recognize speech input. Some allow touch interaction and some allow multitouch interaction. Some will collect data from sensors attached to your body. On the output side, some will have multi-color displays, some will only have two colors, some will have sound, some will vibrate in different ways and some will output data directly to some actuators connected to a person or to some other device.

Understanding the characteristics of the technologies and how they can interact with each other and with people is the beginning of designing a digital space. Some technologies will be carried by people, others will be embedded in the physical environment. Some will communicate only over short distances, while others will communicate over large distances. Some are reliable, some are not. Some need to connect through "line of sight," others can connect and communicate through walls (as long as they are not too thick!). Some use shared communication channels, others have dedicated lines of communication. Some have fast communication and processing abilities and others are rather slow.

Most digital technologies provide some storage space for content. The size of the storage space is important to UX, as is the access to it. There are public, private and shared storage spaces and different types of content that exist in those spaces. Moving content between them, easily and naturally, is critical to providing a good UX.

The input and output abilities of technologies will affect what forms of human-technology interaction are possible. For example to enable gesture-based interaction, the device needs to recognize movement through having a camera, perhaps, or being able to detect through motion sensors. The resolution of a digital display has a critical effect on how people can interact with it. Tangible interaction requires some way of detecting touch and perhaps movement.

Fabrics embedded with digital technologies can detect other interactions such as stroking, scrunching and rubbing. Fabrics can also be manufactured with actuators embedded such as tightening the fabric when a message is received. Ambient displays can provide background information that does not require your full attention. Sensors can tell us what is going on in our "smart cities." The Internet of Things is here and interaction designers will be creating new environments that deliver new experiences whether for artistic, creative or more functional reasons.

Interactive digital technologies are the materials that interaction designers work with. Just as a lighting designer needs to understand lights and a jewelry designer needs to understand the properties of precious stones and metals, so the interaction designer needs to understand the properties of interactive digital technologies and how they work together to produce digital spaces.

4.2   DIGITAL ECOLOGIES

Mark Weiser, the chief scientist at Xerox Palo Alto research Center (PARC), coined the term "ubiquitous computing" in 1988 and published his vision of computing in the 21st century in 1991 (Weiser, 1991). In this he discussed how computers would become embedded in the environment and lying around on the office desk because they would be so ubiquitous. He proposed that these "pads" would be scrap computers, much like scrap paper with no individual identity. He also proposed inch scale computers, "tabs" and large scale displays, "boards." Crucially computers should know where they were; they should know their location. Weiser also proposed the idea of "calm technology" that moved gently from center to periphery, attracting our attention when necessary, then slipping into the background when no longer relevant (Weiser and Seely Brown, 1995).

Building on these ideas Terrenghi et al. (2009) have developed a "geometry of interaction" that includes tabletops, large displays (big enough for a room) and very large displays (for outdoor events) in addition to tabs, pads and boards. They then develop the notion of an ecosystem of displays, people and spaces and discuss the interaction requirements for different types of interaction. One-to-one interaction with pads, for examples could use a "bump together" interaction style for communicating. The interaction of one person with just a few others could be achieved by coupling a tab-sized device to a large screen, thus being able to display what was on the tab-sized device to share it with other people. They also explored different forms of interaction between one, few or many people and the different ecologies that they generated.

Others have taken up this idea of digital device ecologies. In another contribution (Dix et al., 2000) the authors look at location and distance between spaces and at how ecologies are nested in one another. They focus on the importance of location as the main aspect of context-awareness for devices and again look at the number of people involved in the ecology and the physical space for interactions. They discuss how the different infrastructure contexts and the capabilities of different systems in different domains affect the success of interactions. In their model of device ecologies, Dix et al. discuss the spatial qualities of configurations of digital devices. For example there are nearness relations between objects that depend on the number of mouse clicks required to get from one part of the space to another. There are different levels of abstraction to consider, where the designer focuses perhaps on just one device, or on a collection of networked devices or on the performance of the whole ecology. This leads them to consider what is nearby in the space, what things are at the "same location" (and what does that mean in the digital space). They also consider the contribution of personal, group and public spaces and how they work together.

Tim Coughlan and his colleagues provide a detailed review of various ecologies (Coughlan et al., 2012) and what a poor UX is typically experienced. They discuss the trade-off between seamless interaction between devices and seamful interaction. With seamful interaction (Chalmers et al., 2005), users are aware that the technologies do not interact smoothly but use this as a part of the interaction. Rogers also talks about niche ecologies for particular activities, such as providing children with engaging educational outdoor games (Rogers, 2006) and Jung et al. (2008) look at how people classify artifact ecologies. They develop a framework that focuses on the physical, interactional, functional and informational ecological factors involved and on the different layers of ecologies that people perceived. Memarovic et al. (2012) explore the ideas of ecologies in the context of public displays.

In a more theoretical contribution Bødker and Klokmose (2012) use activity theory to look at the mediating effects of artifact ecologies. They identify the different levels at which people assess and make use of artifacts, the activity level (why should I use this artifact), the action level (what do I need to do) and the operational level (how do I use this artifact). We revisit this leveled view of conceptualizing artifacts in Chapter 6. Crabtree and Rodden (2008) also discuss ecologies (drawing upon some of the same experiences as Chalmers) focusing on the fragmented interaction that often occurs as people have to move across interaction with different devices.

Dourish and Bell (2007) point out how an understanding of the digital infrastructure is so important in the age of pervasive computing and how the technological infrastructure (of the digital space) brings another layer to our experiences of physical space. Certainly our experiences of digital space are rarely seamless and most days I find myself having to encounter as present-at-hand (see Chapter 2) the vagaries of wireless communications.

The close commingling of digital and physical space leads to another type of digital ecology, cyber-physical systems. Cyber-physical systems are physical spaces where a digital space (often a wireless sensor network, WSN) is very tightly coupled to a physical space in order to provide certain functionality. For example there are many thousands of sensors in the Pacific Ocean that monitor seismic activity, in order to provide warnings of tsunami. Vineyards may be covered with sensors to detect diseases and insect activity. Cities may be embedded with technologies to monitor air quality. We discuss these new environments in terms of blended spaces in Chapter 9.

Digital space, then, is made up from many digital ecologies that are nested in each other with various degrees of connectivity and ability to share content and transfer content across devices. People move in and out of different ecologies and may be aware or not as they transition from one digital place to another. Even at home it is now very difficult to understand the digital space and to know where some digital content is. If you are watching a movie that is in an iTunes library that is "on" a laptop, played through an Apple TV connected to a regular TV, exactly where is the bit of the movie that you are watching? And where is the rest of it?

4.3   VIRTUAL ENVIRONMENTS

Two particular types of digital space can be considered as virtual worlds, or virtual environments (VEs). The first is where an avatar (typically a graphical representation of the user) is portrayed in a graphical environment and is able to interact with content and with other avatars representing other people. These worlds have been highly popular in computer games where the user's avatar will compete with others, some representing real people, others being computer generated. When I am playing a computer game controlling a virtual character, there is a clear notion that the avatar is in some sense "me." There is a social presence (Section 2.4) that is evoked through the avatars and the strength of this presence is a mark of the quality of the game. In addition to games there are a number of virtual worlds such as Second Life where people's virtual selves can engage in a whole range of social activities.

A second sense of virtual worlds concerns more or less immersive virtual reality (VR). In the most common version of this, a user wears a head-mounted display (HMD) that tracks the movement of their head and displays images—usually graphical, but sometimes photographic—relevant to this head movement. Partly because the user is immersed in the experience and visually cut-off from the rest of the world, the results can be highly engaging and realistic giving a real sense of being in another world. It was the early experiences with such systems that led to the interest in telepresence (see Chapter 2). However, the other side of the experience is that the user feels disembodied and if he or she looks down, they will not see their feet unless a programmer has thought to include some representation of feet in the display.

One of the important aspects of virtual worlds is that there is a real sense of a virtual space and a real sense of moving through the space. VR systems can be augmented with physical features to improve this sense of movement. For example a real treadmill or walkway can be used so that the user actually does walk (though does not travel anywhere in real space) and if this matches the travel through the virtual world that they are in, a strong sense of movement is experienced. An early model of navigation in VR was developed by Steve Benford and Lenart Fahlén that is still relevant today (Benford and Fahlén, 1993). They identified that interaction takes place between people and/or objects through a medium. Every avatar and object in the VE has an aura surrounding them that defines the extent of their presence. When the auras of two objects/avatars come into contact they are able to interact. They also recognized that awareness of others is critical to interaction in VR. They define the focus of an object/avatar as the area around it that enables it to be aware of others and the nimbus of an object/avatar is the area that enables others to be aware if it.

This quite general model has been picked up by others, such as Dix et al. (2000) who use it within their discussion of device ecologies, and it is a description that chimes with our own view of interaction in general. A notion similar to Floridi's levels of abstraction is also present in the model as is our notion of interaction through media. Although not explored in their paper, some philosophical issues of presence are there. The nimbus of an object is where it begins its presencing

(Section 2.5), and the focus is the area that the avatar/object extends outward. Thus we could consider that the focus is concerned with the extensions that people have with respect to some medium.

In a thoughtful self-ethnography of presence in a virtual environment, Maeva Veerapen explores her own experiences using the Second Life VE (Veerapen, 2011). She had experienced a strong sense of presence while moving through Second Life owing to a real-world experience from her childhood. In her paper she explores how the practiced use of the keyboard commands in Second Life enables the practiced user to incorporate the keyboard into their body. As we discussed in Section 2.5, once something is incorporated into the body, the person feels present at the extent of the incorporated artifact. Practiced users tap the commands at a pre-reflexive level. The keyboard is ready-to-hand and hence the user is able to act directly on the content of the keyboard as medium, which is the actions that the avatar makes in the virtual world. Now, if we turn to where the place of the experience happens, the "significant locale" of the experience is not in her office where the real Maeva is sitting, it is in the virtual world. The sense of presence has been emplaced from the physical body to the place of the extended self. The avatar is a prosthesis, an extension of the self into the virtual world. Many accomplished game players will know this experience of feeling a sense of presence of oneself in a virtual world.

Mennecke et al. (2010) also consider presence in virtual worlds and propose an embodied social presence theory. They identify three places that come together to give the feeling of social presence: the physical, the virtual and the imagined. (We return to the idea of the imaged place in Chapter 6 where we discuss conceptual space.) They identify the space where avatars meet in virtual worlds as the place where meanings can be exchanged and feelings identified. In short this is the medium of interaction that we have discussed in Chapter 2 and Benford and Fahlén allude to in their theory. Mennecke et al. argue that achieving this sense of presence in virtual worlds requires five steps. Recognition of the other digital self precedes the recognition of one's own digital self. Collaborative engagement is followed by an appraisal by the assumed real self of the other and a reflection on the digital self in the collaboration.

VEs keep promising to have a big impact on interaction, but continue to remain a relatively niche digital space. The fact that the immersive aspects of the experiences in VEs necessarily mean that the user is cut off from the rest of the world means that VEs provide a very particular experience and seem unlikely to integrate into mixed reality in a natural way.

4.4   DESIGNING DIGITAL SPACE

Designers of digital spaces have a challenging task. They need to understand the range of devices that they have control over. They need to design expecting people will bring certain sorts of devices with them when they enter the space. They need to consider what content is "in" a particular device, or what content can be loaded into a device and how the different bits of content work together. They need to consider how many people will be involved in any particular interaction and whether the interaction is between one person, a few people or many people. They need to consider what different devices know about the context of the interaction. Lieberman and Selker (2000) identify context-aware computing as the device knowing about the physical environment, the person using the device, the state of the computational environment, the activities being undertaken and the history of the human-computer-environment interaction. This last point is particularly difficult to achieve as rarely does a single device keep track of the interaction history, let alone how that can be shared with other devices. Recall the discussion of service design in Chapter 1 and how important it is to have a smooth transition between interactions when they are based around a single service. In the design of more open-ended digital spaces this becomes even more difficult.

Designing interactions is also about allocating functions and content to people or to devices. Designers need to consider the capabilities of people and the constraints on what they can do. People will forget things over time. They will forget things in working memory in a very short time. They are not good at following long lists of instructions, at carrying out boring tasks repeatedly and so on. On the other hand, people are good at improvising and at dealing with ambiguity and incomplete information. On the whole, the capabilities of technology are just the reverse.

But it is not just a question of efficiency. The interaction should be engaging, enjoyable and fulfilling. Moreover, if the system supports working life, it should help to create satisfying and meaningful jobs, while a product for home use has to fit lifestyle and desired image. The idea of "patterns"—perceived regularities in an environment—has been adopted by designers of interactive systems and appears as interaction patterns. As with architectural patterns (see Chapter 3), inter-action patterns can be identified at many different levels of abstraction. For example, there is much good advice on the Apple website for the design of UX on iPads and iPhones. However, the design of digital space as a whole is still very much a craft for interaction designers to learn.

4.5   SUMMARY

Digital spaces are now ubiquitous, going from the apps on a smartphone to a tablet linked to the Internet through a wireless network to gesture-based interaction with large screens. Environments covered in digital technologies that sense certain data and actuate functions are becoming increasingly common. Devices that people can wear that connect with their tablets or phones that sense movement such as golf swing bring experiences that were previously only possible in virtual worlds, using gesture or a wand to interact with a screen, into the real world. More things become connected to the Internet and are brought into the digital space. Homes have a digital space, work has many digital spaces, being on the road has its own digital space and socializing spaces such as cities, cafes and parks have their digital spaces. We can describe digital spaces in terms of the objects that exist, physically and conceptually, and look at the relationships between these objects—how they are configured and interrelated. This is the topology of digital space. We can consider the content of the digital spaces in much the same way. Digital spaces allow people to do certain things (allow for agency), may contain artificial agents and of course they change over time. Digital spaces are volatile.

CHAPTER 5

Information Space

The idea of information space is something that many writers talk about in a fairly casual way. But in this exploration of spaces of interaction, it is worthwhile spending a bit more time exploring the concept. Information space is the space of semiotics. It is where people decode the signs in the world around them and use this information to guide their activities. In terms of Pact the information space lies in the relationship between the P and T on the one hand and the P&T and the A on the other hand. All are influenced by context, of course. Figure 5.1 tries to capture this with the hashed area representing the information space.

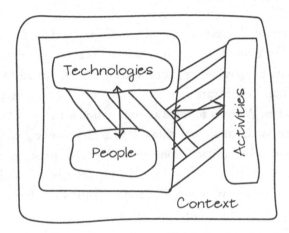

Figure 5.1: Locating the information space in Pact.

We conceptualize the situation as consisting of two types of space. The activity space is the space of real-world activities. It is the space of physical action and physical experiences. In order to undertake activities in the activity space, people need access to information. This is the information space. Much of it is digital of course, but much of it is not. For example people derive a great deal of meaning and information from the physical world (such as archways, doors and street corners) and from the analogue media that is in the physical world such as signposts, shop signs and advertising hoardings. Figure 5.2 tries to capture the role of the information space in bridging the relationship between people and their activities. People make use of information spaces to undertake activities.

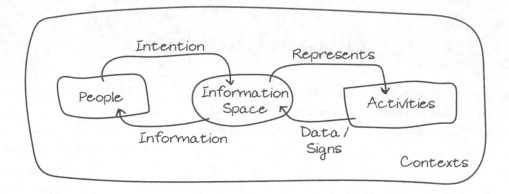

Figure 5.2: Another view of information space.

Information spaces are often created explicitly to provide certain data and certain functions to facilitate some activity. For example a train timetable is created to provide information to help people undertake the activity of traveling by train. A TV guide is created to help people with the activity of watching television. A software application such as iPhoto is developed to help people edit and organize photographs. We refer to these as information artifacts (IAs). An IA is any object that people use to help them understand something or to achieve some goal in their activity space. There are thousands of information artifacts from simple sheets of paper to complex websites. The way that information artifacts are structured and arranged is described by an information architecture. Designers need to understand how to organize and structure the information artifacts in order to make an understandable and usable information space.

In addition to IAs, information spaces may contain agents and devices. Agents are autonomous. People, animals and some software are agents. Devices are objects that do not deal with the derivation of information. They supply simple functions, store data, transmit data from one place to another, or are used to display data. A switch is a device, a screen is a device and a router is a device. Of course we have to bear in mind the level of abstraction when talking about information spaces just as we do when talking about physical spaces, presence and interaction in general. At one level a cable joining a TV to set-top box is a device for transmitting data, but if the TV is not working properly then the cable may be used as an information artifact in the trouble-shooting activity as it is inspected for any sign of damage.

Dörk et al. (2011) invoke the concepts of a flaneur in this discussion of information spaces. A flaneur was a person in the new and emerging cities of 19th-century Europe who enjoyed wandering the city streets and engaging in the aesthetics of the environment without having any other motivating goal. Dörk et al. bring this concept to the activity of finding information. They say,

"Following the flaneur's attitude toward the city, the information flaneur sees beauty and meaning in growing information spaces." They see "striking similarities" between the cities of the 19th century and today's information spaces and discuss how the flaneur moves through the information landscapes of today's technologies. We return to these ideas of the navigation of information space in Chapter 8. In the rest of this chapter we explore the theory and philosophy of information space.

5.1   INFORMATION ARTIFACTS

Information artifacts (IAs) are things that allow people to derive information where information is defined as an "increment of knowledge" or a "difference that makes a difference." IAs consist of many signs that are ordered and structured in some fashion (Green and Benyon, 1996). These signs might be words, icons, groups of signs, colors, sounds, vibrations and so on. In Chapter 2 we introduced semiotics as an important part of the media that people inhabit and discussed how semiotics is used in different areas such as film, product design, advertising and so on. People make meaning from signs by associating the signs with codes and contexts, denotations and connotations and reasoning that something is the case because of the information derived. For example if I look at the weather app on my iPhone and see a display I might infer that it will be sunny at 4pm this afternoon (Figure 5.3).

Figure 5.3: An Information Artefact weather app.

Note that I have to learn certain conventions to decode the signs—for example that it is time along the top and temperature along the bottom. I can scroll left and right by stroking my figure across the screen to see other times. I need to interpret the various icons for different types of weather. The key issue is that *all information artifacts employ various signs, structured in some fashion, and provide functions to manipulate those signs both physically and conceptually*. It is through this interaction that people are able to derive information and different pieces of information will be more or less easily obtained from different information artifacts.

For example, consider a train timetable. I can phone a particular number and listen to a talking timetable, or I can consult a paper timetable. The paper timetable can be physically manipulated by marking it with a pen or conceptually manipulated by scanning for arrival times. These functions are not available with a talking timetable even though the information content may be the same. If I need to be in London before 4:30 P.M. the departure time of the train I need to catch can be easily found on the paper timetable, but with a talking timetable I need to wait until I hear about the train that gets in after 4:30 and then try to recall the departure time of the train before that.

Every information artifact constrains and defines a (very small) information space. Together all these information artifacts make up the information spaces such as apps and websites that we are familiar with. Notice that an IA consists of some conceptual information content and some signs that represent that content and ways of manipulating that content. So the train timetable has content about departure and arrival times, but does not have content about who the driver of the train is. The weather app has content about the weather hour by hour for today, but not for tomorrow. As we see in the next section, deciding on what content to provide in an IA is the job of information architecture.

However, also notice that the signs and functions of an IA constitute the interface to that IA. Being physical the interface is an object in the activity space and hence may have its own IA to enable information to be uncovered about this interface. In this fashion information artifacts are built on top of one another. This is another reason why the level of abstraction is so critical in any discourse about information and interactivity.

5.2   INFORMATION ARCHITECTURE

Information architecture is the design of information spaces. Just as real-world architects have to understand client needs and design appropriate structures to enable those needs to be realized, so information architects have to design the structures that will enable information to be derived. Moreover, information architects need to design information spaces that are enjoyable and effective, for the information flaneur, or indeed anyone looking for information, to inhabit. These structures are realized in the digital space as apps and websites and in the physical space as objects such as maps, signs or physical structures.

As we illustrated in Figure 5.2, the activity space—the space where people undertake activities—has to be represented by data in the information space. The question is then, what data should we choose to represent activities? What information, what content, is going to be useful for people undertaking some activity? For example if I want to visit a historical site, what information is going to provide me with a good experience? Should the information architect provide information on the dates of events that happened there, or information about famous people who visited there, or information about the geography and geology? Should the information architect provide video of past events, links to websites for further information, or an audio guide to provide a tour around the site? Should they provide information boards at key locations, maps of the site, guidebooks, or should they provide all this sort of information on a smartphone app? The information architect is going to provide the structure within which the user experience will unfold.

The first thing they must do, then, is to specify an ontology. An ontology is "a designed conceptualization of some activity" (Gruber, 1995). It is a conceptual model of a domain described in terms of objects (or entities), their relationships and their structure. An information architect analyzes some domain (a sphere of activity, or activity space) and decides on the objects of interest and the relationships between those objects. There is a wealth of research on conceptual modeling dating back to the early days of artificial intelligence, database theory (Sowa, 1995) and now popular in work on the Semantic Web.

The ontology concerns deciding what objects are in the domain and how those objects are structured and related to one another. Finding an appropriate ontology is critical and will affect all the other characteristics of the information space and subsequent UX. For example if an information architect is designing a clothes shopping website the ontology would include objects such as "women's tops," "men's tops," "women's trousers," "women's jackets" and so on. This is the ontology, the way that the physical space and the physical objects are conceptualized. Quite often the information architects of websites come up with quite strange ontologies, which is why you may find it difficult to find certain objects on websites. For example in one well-known clothes shopping site, the term "Levi's," is not recognized by the search engine, nor does it appear under any other category such as "Jeans." The designers of this site have not included "Levi's" in their ontology, so no one can find them! Benyon (Benyon, 2006; 2007) discusses information architecture and website design.

Choosing an appropriate level of abstraction for this is vital as this influences the number of entity (or object) types that there are, the number of instances of each type and the complexity of each object. A coarse-grained ontology will have only a few types of objects each of which will be "weakly typed"—i.e., will have a fairly vague description. This means that the objects will be quite complex and there will be a lot of instances of each type. Choosing a fine-grained ontology results in a structure which has lots of strongly typed, simple objects with a relatively few instances of each. In a fine-grained ontology the object types differ from each other only in some small way; in a coarse-grained ontology they differ in large ways. In the case of the clothes store, the information architect could have chosen to conceptualize the clothes using a much coarser-grained ontology such as "women's wear" instead of identifying women's tops, women's jumpers, etc.

The size of an information space is governed by the number of objects, which in turn is related to the ontology. A larger space will result from a finer-grained ontology, but the individual objects will be simpler. Hence the architecture should support locating specific objects through the use of indexes, clustering, categorization, tables of content and so on. With the smaller space of a coarse-gained ontology the emphasis is on finding where in the object a particular piece of information resides. The objects will be structured into IAs that provide interfaces with particular functions for interacting with the objects. For example if the information architect puts all the objects into a single page on a website, the user will need to scroll down through the page to find the information that they are interested in. If the architect structures the objects into different sections and provides links in a menu on the page, then the user can jump directly to the section they are interested in (provided they share an understanding with the information architect about what that section should be called).

The information architecture of an information space will also impact on the topology of the space, on the distance between objects and on the direction relations between object types and instances. For example the ontology affects the next and previous relations between instances. Is the next item next in chronological order, alphabetical order or some other structure? How close is a particular instance to the current location, or how close, and in which direction do I need to go to get to a different type of object in the space?

A second key characteristic of information space is the volatility. Volatility is concerned with how often the types and instances of the objects change. In general it is best to choose an ontology that keeps the types of object stable. Given a small, stable space, it is easy to invent maps, or guided tours to present the contents in a clear way. But if the space is very large and keeps changing then very little can be known of how different parts of the space are and will be related to one another. In such cases interfaces will have to look quite different.

The third characteristic of information spaces concerns agency; people and artificial agents and what activities can be undertaken. In some spaces, users are on their own and there are no other people about—or they may be about but users do know about them. In other spaces users can easily communicate with other people (or artificial agents) and in other spaces there may not be any people now, but there are traces of what they have done. The availability of agents in an information space is another key feature affecting its usability and enjoyment. Agents also contribute to social navigation of information spaces (see Section 8.3).

The final aspect of an information space concerns the technologies that are used to access and deliver the (information) content. These include all the characteristics of digital technologies discussed in Chapter 4 and non-digital information artifacts. The technologies for content provision, consumption and manipulation have a huge impact on the UX of the information space. For example displays may be large or small, color or monochrome, touch-enabled or not, high-resolution or not. There may be speech as part of the medium as input or output. There may be music and other forms of non-speech sound. There may be gesture recognition, tangible interaction or haptic feedback. There may be video, animation or 3D representations. And there will be different applications, software for the production, consumption, manipulation and transmission of content.

5.3 INFORMATION SPACE AND ACTIVITY SPACE

We have seen that information spaces may include two other types of object in addition to IAs: agents and devices (Benyon, 1998; 2001; 2005). Agents are purposeful. Unlike information artifacts that wait to be accessed, agents are proactive. People are agents and there are artificial agents. For example spell-checkers are agents, alarm clocks are agents and there are increasingly more complex agents such as the bidding agent on eBay. Once an alarm is set it will monitor the time until it is time to ring. Once a spell-checker is turned on it will seek out words that are not in its dictionary, underlining them or automatically correcting them until it is turned off.

Information spaces may also contain devices that are entities that do not deal with the content of signs. They transfer or translate signs without dealing with meanings. Things such as buttons, switches, network connections and displays are devices.

The relationship between information spaces and activity spaces is illustrated in Figure 5.4. The activity space consists of activities, but overlaid on these are the information space(s) that are constituted by a network of agents (A), information artifacts (IA) and devices (D). The illustration is intended to emphasize that a single activity is rarely supported by a single information artifact. Accordingly people have to move across and between the agents, information artifacts and devices in order to undertake their activities. They have to navigate the information space.

To further complicate matters, related information artifacts delivered across different media necessarily have to assume different forms and structures at different levels of use. For example, a paper timetable is structured in a manner to suit the nature of paper and its "handiness." The arrivals and departures board in the station is structured in such a way as to suit a simple dot-matrix display system that operates at a distance, and CRT monitors on the station platforms shift between lists of arrivals and the current arriving train in a way that only screen-based media will allow. Each of these artifacts overlaps with the other but different media require different design techniques and more often than not, these different artifacts are designed by different people at different times resulting in different conceptualizations of the information to be presented. This can make it harder for people to make sense of them, as they all have to work in concert in order to be sensible.

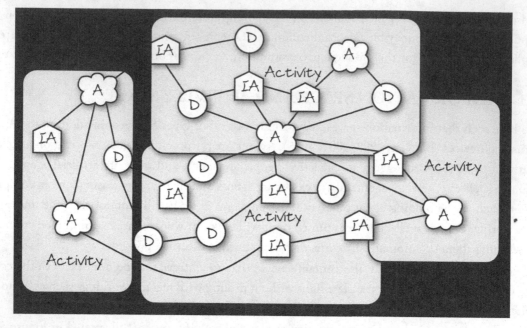

Figure 5.4: Conceptualization of information space and activities.

5.4   SUMMARY

The most ubiquitous information spaces nowadays are probably smartphone apps. Designers see an opportunity to gather information about some activity and organize and present it as an app. So there are apps for checking the weather, tracking buses, trains and flights, finding restaurants in cities and a whole multitude of other activities. But designers only have control over the information architecture of the apps they are designing. Frequently they rely on someone else's information space to provide data for their apps. So the interface between information spaces becomes a critical part of the overall UX.

Information spaces span the digital and physical, but they can also be described in terms of the ontology, topology, volatility and agency that they contain. The information architecture will define the way that an activity is conceptualized in terms of data objects and hence what people need to know to make meaning through interacting with it. Information spaces form an important part of the medium of interaction (Chapter 2).

CHAPTER 6

Conceptual Space

The conceptual space is where people understand things. It is where they form intentions to do things and work out how to change their environment. It is also where people imagine. In Chapter 2 we described people as existing in a medium that extends out in many different directions to a greater or lesser degree. So, the conceptual space is not simply in people's heads. Certainly people will need to think about things in their heads, but they will use the objects that are in the world, the design of the physical space and interactions with the digital, informational and the physical in order to conceptualize things. Designers need to look at how people conceptualize their media and try to design so that people can understand what interactions are possible and how they can have the best UX. For example in Chapter 4 we discussed how not knowing where a streaming video actually is delivers a poor UX. When the video stops playing and a little icon goes whirring round and round, having a good conceptualization of the space will help to avoid the frustration of not knowing what is going on.

Part of understanding what opportunities there are for action in a space is knowing how to classify and categorize things in a sensible way. In Chapter 5 we discussed information architecture. Developing an information architecture that maps well onto how people conceptualize an activity requires designers to develop an ontology that people will understand; and that requires an understanding of classification.

Finally the conceptual space is where people undertake creative thought. Conceptual blending is a theory of creativity and thought that brings together the embodied nature of cognition with reflective thinking.

6.1 MENTAL SPACES

The idea that people develop mental models of things has long been at the center of cognitive theory (Johnson-Laird, 1983). Mental models have been particularly popular in HCI where applied cognitive psychology can be brought to bear on interaction design. The theory is that people will form mental models of devices and interactions and use these to guide their behavior. Frequently these models will be inaccurate, or will be incomplete or will not reflect what actually happens. The theory continues that we can "run" a mental model when required. For example if I ask you how many windows there are in your house or flat you will probably have to mentally count them by imagining that you are in the room. This is because this is not the sort of information you usually get asked for, and so it cannot be just retrieved. Similarly you can imagine a trip to work and describe where you went and where you crossed the road by running your mental model of the activity.

However, as we have seen in Chapter 2, being human is not just like that. Much of our knowledge is in the world in the form of signs, symbols and information artifacts. Moreover the things that are in the world affect our conception of the world. When we imagine how to get from one place to another, the existence of the roads affects how we conceptualize things. It is also the case that mental models are not the only form of knowledge that people have.

Phil Turner provides a detailed account of the various ways that people deal with the world without relying on mental models that he terms "coping" (Turner, 2013). Drawing on the work of Heidegger and other philosophers and the idea that as humans we are being-in-the-world, coping is the "absorbed engagement" with technology. We deal with technologies will little or no conscious effort. This is also known as tacit knowledge (Polyani, 1983)—knowing how to do something naturally without necessarily knowing facts about it. This is practiced knowledge such as being able to ride a bike, drive a car or, so the suggestion goes, answer e-mail.

More conscious reflective thinking can be useful when interacting with any complex device, particularly if users are engaged in trouble shooting when things have not worked out as they expected. Daniel Dennett (1996) calls these different "stances." We can understand the behavior of complex systems by taking a physical stance, a design stance or an intentional stance. With the physical stance the observer determines the physical constitution and the physical nature of any exchange of signals or data between the systems. The observer can then predict the outcome of an interaction based on physical and biological laws. For example if a bicycle does not work you can look at the cogs and the chain and see if anything is stuck. With digital technologies, this is much more difficult of course because you cannot see the inner workings.

However, we might also want to look at interactions taking a design stance. With this strategy, an observer predicts how the systems will interact by believing that the interaction will be as it was designed. The design stance looks at interaction from the conceptual level. It is the level of description familiar to all of us when we try to work out how to do something with an interactive system. "Press that icon over there and then X should happen."

However, only designed behavior is predictable from the design stance. If a different sort of analysis is required then people may adopt the intentional stance. This perspective on interaction involves considering what the interaction will be like if the systems behave as if they were rational agents. Using the intentional stance enables observers to consider interactions from the perspective of what the logical things to do are if you want to achieve some outcome in a particular setting. For example the design of an interactive system that includes a large button on a screen that says "press here to start" could reasonably be considered a good design if the person interacting with it wants to start some process. The design maps onto the intentions of user. Zenon Pylyshyn agrees that what "might be called the basic assumption of cognitive science [is] that there are at least three distinct, independent levels at which we can find explanatory principles biological, functional and intentional" (Pylyshyn, 1986, p. 131). The levels are distinguishable from each other and necessary because they reveal generalizations that would otherwise not be apparent. Activity Theory as we saw with Bødker and Klokmose's (2012) treatment of device ecologies (Section 4.2) also adopts this idea of three levels of description.

Another approach to conceptualizing interactions comes from the work of Jens Rasmussen's work and the work of Kim Vicente. Rasmussen (1986) discusses the different levels of knowledge that people may employ at the different levels of abstraction. Skills are employed at the physical level of interaction where practiced understanding and tacit knowledge are used. Rules come into play when considering the design stance and how interactions generally work. Knowledge is required to deal with the intentional level knowing what external entities can be used to achieve certain goals.

The work of Rasmussen and Vicente appears under the title of Ecological Interface Design (EID, Vicente and Rasmussen, 1992) or Cognitive Work Analysis. EID describes a system, subsystem or component at five levels of abstraction. At the top level is the system's purpose; the analysis takes an intentional stance. Taking the design stance, EID distinguishes between the abstract function and the generalized function of the system. The abstract function concerns the capabilities that it must have in order to achieve its purpose, and the generalized function describes the links between the physical characteristics and that abstract function. At the physical level of description EID distinguishes the physical function from the physical form of the system. This means-ends hierarchy provides a powerful analytic technique for understanding how systems function.

For example, a car's purpose is to transport people along a road. Therefore it must have the abstract functions of some form of power, some form of accommodating people and some form of wheels. These abstract functions may be provided by the generalized functions of a petrol engine, some seats and some wheels with pneumatic tires. Physically the engine might be realized as an eight-cylinder fuel-injected engine, the seats are of a size to accommodate people and the tires have an ability to take the weight of the car and its passengers. The physical forms of these functions are the features that distinguish one type of car from another and concern the different arrangements of the engine components, the color and material of the seats and the characteristics of the tires.

It is fair to say that even though we believe cognition to be embodied and embedded and distributed in the world, there is still a place for mental models and mental spaces where conscious, considered thinking gets done. In the early days of cognitive theory these mental models were described in terms of abstract symbols that represented objects in the world. But, as we discussed in Chapter 2, thanks to the work of Lakoff and Johnson (1980) the bodily basis of our mental models is now recognized. Recall that they point to the importance of bodily-based image schemata as the foundation of cognition.

The take-home message for designers of interactive systems is that they need to help people develop a good mental model of some interaction. This will be achieved if designers pay attention to the conceptual model of the system they are developing to ensure that it is clear and understandable. Recognize that people will bring their previous experiences with them, so design to scaffold any new ideas or interactions using those. Design to exploit basic image schemata and common ways of working.

In HCI and interaction design these ideas have been applied with various degrees of success over a number of years. John Waterworth described his design of "Schema space" in his chapter in (Höök et al., 2003) where he applied the path and center-periphery schemas to website design and there is a lot of discussion of metaphors and image schemata in Imaz and Benyon (2007). More recently Jorn Hurtienne et al. (2008) have explored the use of image schemas in tangible interaction design and have continued to apply the method in a number of settings. Their work provides some compelling evidence that user experience is improved if designers make use of an understanding of conceptual metaphor in their designs (Löffler et al., 2014).

One persistent area of argument is whether there are natural mappings that should be exploited. For example Apple changed the way that scrolling worked when they moved to their Mountain Lion operating system so that it was consistent with how scrolling worked on the iPad, arguing that this was a more natural mapping. I consistently make mistakes when navigating the channels on my electronic TV guide because I think I should go up from Channel 2 to Channel 1 because it appears first on the display, so I press the "up" arrow on the remote control. The system requires me press the down arrow because 1 is less than 2.

6.2   CATEGORIES

We discussed the importance of information architecture in Chapter 5. In addition to deciding on the ontology suitable to represent a domain, information architects need to consider how to group things together into categories. There are some useful techniques such as card sorting that information architects and designers can use to help understand the categories that their users utilize, but there is also some background theory that is useful.

George Lakoff considers how we classify things in his classic book *Women, Fire, and Dangerous Things* (Lakoff, 1997). The title of this book reflects the fact that an Australian Aboriginal tribe has these things in the same category, something that other cultures might find surprising. In this book Lakoff discusses the idea of basic level categories of objects and how they too are derived from bodily experience.

Basic level categories are "basic" from a perceptual point of view, a functional point of view and a cultural view. For example chairs and tables would be basic level categories, but furniture would be too abstract and different types of chairs or tables—three-legged tables or chairs and stools, say—would be too concrete. We cannot easily draw a picture or otherwise perceive a category such as furniture. Basic level categories are associated with general motor experiences and general cultural functions. We have general motor programs for using chairs and tables, but not for using furniture in general. Basic level categories are defined by how we interact with the world given the bodies we have, our cognitive models and our culturally defined purposes.

Recall the discussions on levels of abstraction in Chapter 1 and how important it is for designers to get these right. In Chapter 5 we discussed the ideas of information architecture and the need to find an ontology that is suitable for users to understand, as opposed to some classification that designers can understand. An important message from the idea of basic level categories is that they are culturally dependent. Interaction designers come from a different culture from the users of their systems, because they are accustomed to thinking about interaction everyday. For designers, understanding the categories used by users will help them to design at a human scale.

Eleanor Rosch has also developed a theory of categories and shown that there is no simple objective classification of things (Rosch, 1976). Instead people classify objects in terms of prototype theory. This theory argues that people group things based on their "family resemblances," the attributes that they have in common. However, finding categories that withstand the test of time can be challenging. Umberto Eco discusses the trouble that 19th-century scientists had in classifying the platypus (Eco, 1997) and even today biologists use multiple classification systems for plant taxonomies.

6.3   METAPHOR AND BLENDS

A third aspect of the conceptual space that is important for interaction design concerns how designers can help people to understand new concepts, new ideas and new forms of interaction. It is here that the use of conceptual metaphor and conceptual blends can be useful.

Metaphor is taking concepts from one domain (called the source domain, or the vehicle) and applying them to another (called the target, or tenor). Recall your schooldays and how you studied "The ship ploughed through the waves," or "The President marshaled his arguments to defend his position." The first of these likens a ship moving through the sea to a plough moving through a field. It suggests the waves are like the furrows. It has connotations of strength and how the ship is pushing aside the sea. For some people it connotes speed of movement. In the second we see arguments likened to a battle, arguments being marshaled as if they were soldiers, the President's position being analogous to a castle or other physical place that needs defending.

In the development of interactive systems we are constantly trying to describe a new domain (a new application, a different design, new interactive facilities) to people. So we have to use metaphor to describe this new domain in terms of something that is more familiar. Blackwell (2006) gives a comprehensive treatment of the role of metaphor in interactive systems design. After a while the metaphorical use of a term becomes entrenched in the language to such an extent that people forget it ever was a metaphor. The functions of "cut" and "paste" that are so common in apps originally came because the early word processors were likened to the process that journalists used to use to layout newspapers. Nowadays this metaphorical root is forgotten and people understand the terms as software functions.

Metaphor is fundamental to the way we think. As we have seen, Lakoff and Johnson (1980; 1999) argue that all our thinking starts from the metaphorical use of a few basic concepts, or "image schemas," such as containers, links and paths that are based in physical experience. A container has an inside and an outside and you can put things in and take things out. This is such a fundamental concept that it is the basis of the way that we conceptualize the world. A path goes from a source to a destination. The key to this philosophy (often called experientialism) is that these basic concepts are grounded in spatial experiences. There are other basic "image schemas" such as front–back, up–down and center–periphery from which ideas flow. Taken with the ideas of basic level categories these ideas provide a powerful basis for designing interactions that people will naturally understand.

Over the last 15 years or so this simple view of metaphor has been developed into the more complex idea of a blend, sometimes called conceptual integration. Gilles Fauconnier and Mark Turner (2002) introduced their ideas on blending in 2002 arguing what we call "metaphors" in design are really *blends*. Rather than projecting concepts from a source domain to a target domain, a blend blends these together into a new space that has new properties not possessed necessarily by either of the input spaces. In addition blending theory recognizes that there is a more generic space that underlies both the input spaces. The blended space may go on to be the input to other blends and in this way complex networks of ideas can be elaborated.

Figure 6.1 illustrates this idea of a blend and how it differs from metaphor theory. The blend that results from bringing two domains together in this way will have some features that were not in the original domains. Blends have an *emergent structure* that results from bringing two sets of concepts (from the source and target domains) together. For metaphors and blends to work, there must be some correspondences between the domains that come from a more generic, or abstract, space. So, for example, the metaphor "the ship ploughs through the waves" works, but the metaphor "the ship ran through the forest" does not. In the second of these there is not sufficient correspondence between the concepts in the two domains. Of course the generic space is itself a domain and hence may itself be using metaphorical concepts. This process works its way back until we reach the fundamental image schemas that are core to our thinking. These include the container, path, link and others such as colors (red is hot, blue is cool, red is stop, green is go) and those bodily schemas that come from experience and perception (up, down, in, out, central, peripheral, etc.).

Ed Hutchins (2005) points to the importance of the "material anchor" for blends. He uses blending theory to look at the relationship between mental models and physical artifacts. He gives the example of people queuing for theatre tickets. Here people use their bodies to represent the position in the queue and the various cultural features that are associated with that (such as not "jumping" the queue). A line of people is not necessarily a queue, but a line of people blended with the concept of a trajectory is a queue.

One way of thinking about metaphors and other expressions is to see them as providing instructions to create and relate mental spaces. The concept of mental space refers to partial cognitive structures that emerge when we think, talk and act about domains. Mental spaces may be linked to one another by connectors that establish relations. The correspondences between domains establish mappings between elements of one space and elements of another. Figure 6.1 illustrates the idea of conceptual blending.

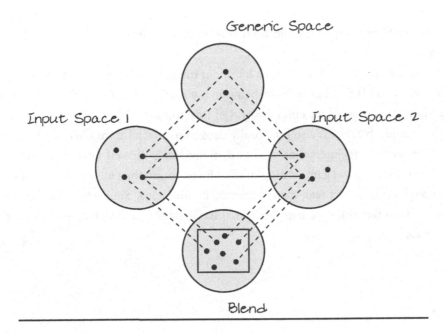

Figure 6.1: Conceptual blending.

There is a very large body of work on embodied cognition and how basic experiences of people being-in-the-world lead to the ways that we think, act and understand. Those interested in the application of conceptual blending should look at Mark Turner's website. This work is important for interaction design because interaction designers are constantly trying to introduce new ideas and new concepts to people. As we will see in Chapter 9, blending enables us to design for new spaces of interaction.

6.4   SUMMARY

The conceptual space is where people do their thinking when they are not using technologies in a ready-to-hand way, i.e., where they are not engaged in absorbed coping (Turner, 2013). In short the conceptual space is where people are looking at a technology as present-at-hand. When you enter an unfamiliar room, or navigate through an unfamiliar city, try to use an interface that you have not used for a while or undertake some activity that you have not done for a while, you will need the conceptual space. If you encounter a breakdown in operation of some device or system then you will need to go through a diagnostic process as suggested in the ecological interaction design analysis. The conceptual space is not a fixed logical space. It is a space for creativity and invention and we constantly create new meanings and classifications through conceptual blending to understand new situations, new interactions and new interfaces. We also project from one domain to another to see things in different contexts, projections that are more effective if they are tied down with a "material anchor."

Mental spaces are also where we do a lot of our imagining. If we play an absorbing computer game, or put on an HMD and experience being in a virtual environment, or indeed if we get engaged in reading a good book, we enter a world of imagination. This aspect of conceptual space is potentially very enjoyable, but is also potentially dangerous. Recall from Chapter 2 how important the sense of presence is to interaction and to distinguishing the self from one's environment. If people get drawn in to a good game sitting in their living room, then all is probably fine, but if they believe the imagined is in fact real, then there may be problems. Similarly if they disbelieve some interaction that is in fact real—perhaps because it has a game-like interface—then again problems are likely to arise.

CHAPTER 7

Social Space

Humans are social creatures and frequently the whole point of engaging in an interaction is to interact with other people to communicate with them or collaborate with them on some activity. However, people do like our privacy at other times and may feel uncomfortable if others get too close or when they are in certain social situations. Nowadays, of course, there is a huge amount of social media that exists to provide new ways to communicate and new ways to for people to present themselves to friends and work colleagues. In this chapter we look at the key features of social space (which we take to include cultural aspects) that impact on interaction design.

Malcolm McCullough (2005) introduces the idea of service ecologies and how important it is to have a good mix of services in the local neighborhood such as a take-away restaurant, hardware store and supermarket. Continuing the idea of ecology, Jodi Forlizzi (2007) introduces social ecology theory in the context of interaction design. This theory focuses on the complex relationships between people and their physical and social environment at different levels of abstraction; micro (individuals and small groups), mesa (neighborhoods) and macro (populations). Forlizzi brings this analysis to bear on digital ecologies (see Section 4.2) highlighting how different methods of analysis can contribute to understanding digital ecologies from a sociological perspective.

Of course we will only scratch the surface of social spaces in this chapter. Anthropologists, cultural commentators and sociologists are the experts who study social phenomena. For example Genevieve Bell is an anthropologist who has been working with interaction design theorist Paul Dourish over several years. In their book they provide a number of very rich descriptions of interaction in many different social spaces across many different cultures. Dourish and Bell (2007) provide a discussion of interaction design and infrastructures. They conclude:

> "The first, and most fundamental, conclusion is that space is organized not just physically but culturally; cultural understandings provide a frame for encountering space as meaningful and coherent, and for relating it to human activities."

In this chapter we look at the key social activities of communication, collaboration and the social spaces of home, work and leisure.

7.1 COMMUNICATION AND COLLABORATION

Social interaction begins with the ability to communicate which we do by expressing our thoughts and emotions through the various media that we have to make things manifest (see Section 2.5). Most obviously communication utilizes speech and language expressed through the medium of sound, but there are also important non-verbal communications that take place through body movement, gestures, posture, facial expression and prosody (the tone, rhythm and pitch of speech). These social signals are a vital part of interaction and help people to establish a common ground for communication (Monk, 2008).

Common ground is the set of shared understandings of the context of some interaction. People are aware of others and the artifacts or objects they are talking about and there is a shared context. In face-to-face conversations people can see what others are doing, but in technology-mediated conversations the common ground needs to be established. Mobile phone conversations often start off with "Hello. Where are you?" to establish some basic shared context.

As we mentioned in Chapter 3, people's use of space, proxemics, is an important aspect of our social space. Proxemics concerns two main areas: physical territory and personal territory. If one person is sitting behind a desk in a formal or semi-formal setting, then this establishes a power relationship. The person on the other side of a desk may feel intimidated, for example. Similarly if our personal space is compromised we may turn away, decrease eye contact or shift position.

In Chapter 2 we introduced the idea of presence and how important it is for people to distinguish between themselves and their environment. A good sense of presence will enable people to feel that they are acting directly on the content of some medium. When this feeling concerns other people it is described as social presence. Social presence varies from the intimacy of naked contact with other people to the immediacy of sitting alongside someone to being in the same room. Awareness is a key aspect of social presence as is the notion of connectedness.

Various technologies can be used to provide a sense of presence for those who are at a physical distance from one another. Things like phones, video-conferencing, Skype and large screen high fidelity displays provide different amounts of social presence.

In addition to one-to-one communications, people will often engage in group working, or they will participate in social groups. The life span of a group is often presented in terms of four key stages: forming, storming, performing, norming. Some shared issue will lead to the formation of a group. Storming refers to how conflicts between individuals and rules are established. Performing describes the stage when the group is most effective and results in norming when conflicts have been resolved and there is a stable coherent group. Of course there are differences between these stages if the group is operating face-to-face or and various techniques need to be used to help the development of healthy long-lasting groups.

People may behave differently in groups because they can take on board the characteristics of the group. Some people may be "social loafers" and allow others to do all the work. Sometimes members of a group all finish up sharing the same ideas, because the group reinforces particular viewpoints. This "group think" can be quite detrimental to a group operating successfully when a degree of discussion and argument is important.

7.2   SOCIAL MEDIA

There are hundreds of different forms of social networking and social media and most people make use of one of them. Facebook is the most ubiquitous in the Western world, providing a simple mechanism for people to post comments and other media for their friends to consume. People can comment on media and comment on the comments of others. In this way Facebook creates a new medium for communication and sharing. With Twitter people post short messages concerning what they are doing. Twitterers are able to follow the messages ("tweets") of other twitterers. Many of these are simply messages such as "having coffee in Oxford," or "lost in Boston," but many other uses have been found for it. Terrorist attacks have become news first on Twitter, as have plane disasters and other events. Businesses use twitter to promote their interests. Of course there are millions of people using Twitter and a plethora of twitter help sites have grown up.

There are also a number of professional social networking sites such as LinkedIn, Pulse and Namyz. These allow people to present their profile for their professional life. Increasingly these sites add new applications. For example LinkedIn allows for sharing PowerPoint files and has common interest groups, with regular updates. There are also companies that provide software that allows people to add social networking to their own sites. This allows topic-specific social networks. For example Freshnetworks.com provides a bundle of "social media" tools that allow programmers to create member profiles, news feeds, ratings and reviews. People can add their own content and edit that of others.

There are now thousands of community websites and social networking environments. Some of these revolve around travel, such as TripAdvisor, others focus on activities such as hiking or cycling, or knitting (ravelry.com). Others focus on finding the best pizza in a new town, the best bars and restaurants, or the best bookshops. Indeed, there are online communities covering almost all hobbies, interests and social issues. Setting up and maintaining an online community is not always straightforward and achieving a critical mass of people with an on-going shared interest can be difficult. In this, online groups share many of the issues of group formation that were discussed earlier. These include getting a critical mass of people, keeping things up to date and knowing how old some advice is.

The social media space continues to evolve at a very fast pace, having a huge impact in some environments and a very small impact in others. Designers need to understand the importance of social media for the people they are designing for and integrate into the other aspects of the interactivity that they are designing. Different channels of social media will require different media forms. Recall from Chapter 2 the maxim "the medium is the message" and nowhere is this more true than in social media. Designers need to choose a suitable medium (short text, video clip, website, longer video and so on) for their message and deliver that through a suitable social media platform. Often designers will need to develop several pieces of social media so that, for example, a short tweet will contain a link to a video clip and include a link to a longer video on YouTube. Designers need to be clear about what they are trying to achieve—raising awareness, selling something, motivating their users, etc.—and the use suitable media to achieve it. Recall the idea of service design discussed in Chapter 1. Designers need to think where they are in the customer journey and how effective the design of social media can be to properly support people.

7.3   DESIGNING THE SOCIAL SPACE

In addition to designing and integrating social media into the overall UX, designers need to consider the social side of the physical spaces they are designing and the inherently social nature of interaction design. Designers can learn a lot from work that has been done in computer supported cooperative working (CSCW) over the years and about how best to design social spaces both for collocated and remotely connected activities (Ackerman, 2000). From our own experience and from the published reports of others, five design themes have emerged that provide a way of structuring the issues that designers of social spaces need to deal with. We discuss the issues in terms of territoriality, awareness, control, interaction and transitions; the Tacit framework.

7.3.1   THE TACIT FRAMEWORK

Territoriality concerns spaces and the relationships between people and spaces. In the context of tabletop interaction, Scott and Carpendale (2010) identify personal spaces, group spaces and storage spaces as important territories. They also point to the importance of orientation, positioning and proximity in addition to the partitioning of spaces into different regions. Territory is also important on large multiuser displays (Peltonen et al., 2008). In co-located collaborative work issues of territoriality are important to the way groups are formed, configuring and reconfiguring their spatial relations depending on the task. There is often a close connection between the control of physical space in the environment and the control of screen workspace, which in turn affects the assignment of roles and tasks. In earlier contributions to collaborative spaces, Buxton (2009) describes media space in terms of the person space, task space and reference space and provides a number of design guidelines for ensuring quality spaces. It is the intersection of these and the ease of moving between them that is important.

Awareness of others and what they are doing is a central issue for the design of social spaces. The concept of awareness hides a large amount of complexity. Awareness includes aspects of attention and focus, so explicit awareness of what others have done is also an important aspect. Different activities invite different degrees of awareness. In a relatively small physical space, people are able to see and hear each other, in larger spaces writing on whiteboards enhances awareness and collaboration and allows people to use gestures to refer to specific objects or the organization of objects on the surfaces. Different surfaces support collaboration through awareness differently, e.g., working around a table creates a higher degree of shared awareness and collaboration.

Control refers both to the control of the software systems and to social control of the collaborative activity. The locus of control is closely related to the access points provided by the technology. Control, and people's understanding of what they can control is key to ideas of appropriation and "tailoring culture." People need to adapt, and shape the environment, the interactions, the content and the computational functions that are available to suit their ways of working. However, this is easier said than done. People have to be confident and capable to appropriate their technological spaces. They need a conceptual understanding of the digital and physical spaces (see Chapter 6) so that they can change their ways of working, and designers need to design to support appropriation and the formation of an appropriate conceptualization of the space.

Interaction concerns how people interact with each other and how they interact with the activities they are undertaking and the technologies that they have. Interaction is one of the four components in the model of collaboration discussed by O'Hara et al. (2011) along with work, communication and service. They emphasize the importance of getting the granularity of the space right. The interplay between the spatial configuration, the social organization and interaction is critical.

Transitions between spaces and between the physical and the digital are important aspects of the social space. Rogers (2006) describes these transitions in terms of access points, or entry points. They find that people are excluded from equitable participation in collaborative activities because of difficulties in gaining access to the physical environment, or the digital environment or both, or in moving between the physical and the digital. In the Shared Information Space framework they offer advice on removing barriers to access and enabling entry points that provide a good overview of the space and the opportunities to move between locations in the spaces.

7.3.2 WORK

The social space of work has been studied from many different perspectives particularly in CSCW (Ackerman, 2000). Here ethnographic studies have informed our understanding of communication and collaboration, which helped to give us the five themes of Tacit. In his analysis of the different types of spaces that can be found at work that demand different social, physical, and technological solutions, McCullough finds 11 situations. He distinguishes places for thinking, presenting, collaborating, negotiating, referencing, officiating, crafting, associating, learning, cultivating and watching. He discusses the social issues in these different situations and where face-to-face interaction is preferred against technology-mediated interaction. For example in negotiating it is often best to have a face-to-face meeting initially in order to establish relationships using the full range of social signals that cannot be transmitted digitally. Issues of presentations will be different depending on the number of people involved (recall the device ecologies discussed by Terrenghi et al. in Chapter 4).

7.3.3   HOME

The home is a complex environment, designed for general use but shaped by individual needs and desires. It is a place often shared by several people with different demands and requirements. It is a place embedded with technologies utilized at various times by people in diverse ways. Until recently most home technologies have been primarily functional; aimed at easing domestic chores such as cooking, washing and cleaning. In the last few years information and communication technologies have added to the technological complexity of the home. Entertainment technologies have become increasingly dominant, as the simple TV has given way to video, DVD and satellite or cable services. Technologies converge and diverge to create new hybrid experiences. Moreover in the future ubiquitous and ambient computing devices and functions will become hidden and communications between devices will become more complex.

In our own work in this area Baillie and Benyon (2008) identified four spaces in the home: private leisure spaces where householders relaxed watched TV, played games, chatted, etc.; public leisure spaces where householders entertained visitors to their homes; communication spaces where telephone(s), telephone directories, personal address books and calendars were located; work spaces where a space was considered or viewed by one or more participants as a place where work activities were carried out. Others have also identified various spaces in the home. Venkatesh et al. (2003) distinguishes social and technological space, but how useful such distinctions are in this rapidly changing environment is a moot point. Certainly in my home all calendars, address books and other items for managing domestic life are now online and places that once held birthday cards and other personal communications are now empty, replaced by Facebook "likes."

7.3.4   LEISURE

Under this broad heading we can consider some of the aspects of places that designers will need to support. In his typology, McCullough has two categories "on the town" and "on the move." In "on the town" he looks at places for gathering, for being seen (recall the "information flaneur" in Chapter 5), for belonging, shopping, playing sport, attending cultural productions and commemorating. His classification of "on the move" distinguishes places for being a tourist, for staying in hotels, for having adventures, driving and walking. Of course, our social activities can be divided up in many different ways and cultural differences feature significantly as emphasized by Dourish and Bell (2007). It is interesting that McCullough has a place for driving but no place for traveling by train, for example.

One area of particular interest for interaction designers is in the development of interactive spaces such as museums and the wide range of pervasive and interactive games. There are many "responsive environments" designed to create cultural and artistic experiences. Lucy Bullivant (2006) surveyed the scene in 2006 under headings such as "interactive building skins" and "intelligent walls and floors," titles that give some understanding to the range of environments that designers are now creating. Her website at urbanista.org has many examples of new technologies and urbanism.

Steve Benford and his colleagues have been working with creative artists and theme park designers to understand how technologies can enhance player and spectator experiences. In Benford et al. (2011) they provide a detailed ethnographic study of one particular public spectacle, Day of the Figurines. Their study emphasizes performativity as a key aspect of interaction. In their discussion they highlight the importance of the Tacit principles, of entry points helping with transitions between spaces and the tabletop supporting awareness. They distinguish transitions that are primarily to entice people in (entry points) and access points that enable them to interact. They also discuss the way that experiences are carefully crafted in these situations to create a coherent ecology. They refer to Genevieve Bell's notions of liminality (by which she means an experience standing apart from everyday life), sociality and engagement of "cultural ecologies" that she developed after undertaking an ethnographic study of a number of museums. They also emphasize how people move through the ecology taking different trajectories. There are the canonical trajectories that designers have created, participant trajectories describing personal journeys and historical trajectories that participants have taken before. These trajectories pass through "hybrid ecologies of space, time, roles and interfaces" that define the experience. Once again they emphasize the importance of the transitions in these trajectories and differentiate the collaborative and individual nature of different interactions. They also stress how important it is to have a coherent design for the interactions with individual artifacts, local ecologies and the overall experience.

Eva Hornecker and her colleagues (e.g., Hornecker and Burr, 2006) have been designing and evaluating interactive museums for several years. They emphasize the social aspects of such interactions where visitors are frequently family groups, so there is a need to have interactivity that appeals to different age groups. Tangible interaction, for example, is better for group activities and tabletops are better for collaboration. Creation of personal content is important and providing opportunities for people to role-play also contributes to an engaging experience.

7.4   SUMMARY

Looking at the social space gives us a different perspective on spaces of interaction, turning away from issues of individuals trying to understand some interface to seeing how people communicate and work, live and play with others. We can see how the physical and digital spaces—in very different settings—need to be configured to support social activity.

Principals for joining groups and collaborating and sharing with others are important in work, home and leisure spaces alike. The way that technologies can deliver better forms of social presence of friends is changing all the time. For example the Nike cycling computer will post real-time data about someone's cycle ride onto their Facebook page. If someone clicks the "like" button on Facebook, the cycle rider hears a cheer in his or her headphones.

Social space is about awareness of others, shared spaces and private spaces, control over what is shown and what is not, the interactions between people and how people transition between spaces to get access to the digital and physical spaces they are after. Social media is making a huge contribution to the rapid evolution of social engagement. Every year when the family visits we use a different combination of apps to keep in touch and plan our joint activities. Social spaces are about the changing nature of engagement as we move through the narrative and physicality of experiences.

CHAPTER 8

Navigating Space

Our consideration of spaces so far has said very little about what people do in those spaces. We have seen that Benford and his colleagues describe the trajectories of experiences (Section 7.3) through ecologies (Section 4.3) and in Chapter 1 we saw how service design is concerned with the whole customer journey (Section 1.4). In Chapter 2 we looked at how the medium of interaction entails both physical and semiotic components and in Section 7.1 we have looked at personal space and how people work in groups.

In this chapter we focus on people in spaces and on how people move through spaces. Perception is concerned with how people sense their environment. Navigation is concerned with how people move through an environment. We have discussed the difference between the designer's creation of spaces and users' tactics of using spaces, the tactics of space (de Certeau, 1984). People's ability to perceive an environment depends on the extensions that they have in terms of technologies and other media and to what extent they have a sense of presence; of places and of others. The nature of the environment in turn affects how effective different forms of perception will be. Furthermore as people we leave marks and traces in our environment, so moving through an environment changes that environment. Benford et al. (2011) distinguish between their continuous trajectories and structures with interconnected but discrete elements. They stress that UX is concerned with the journey, rather than the destination. However, we recognize that people move in and out of their trajectories, through the transitions of access and entry points. We also suggest that not arriving at a destination may upset some people who do want to get somewhere specific, so we think that wayfinding is an important aspect of human existence.

Spatial ability concerns the ability of people to engage in a variety of spatial activities, and it differs quite significantly between individuals. One ability that is often a component in psychological tests is the ability to mentally rotate objects. People are asked to look at an object and match it up with the object that has been rotated. Other aspects of spatial ability include map reading, drawing maps and making judgments about spaces such as estimating distance and direction. It is important for designers to recognize that these individual differences exist in their users and can be quite significant. Designers should design to support those with poorer spatial ability by providing environmental cues, maps and directions that make it easier to navigate (on individual differences see, e.g., Gruszka et al., 2010).

8.1   NAVIGATION

Navigation is concerned with finding out about, and moving through, an environment. It includes three different but related activities (Benyon and Höök, 1997).

- Object identification, which is concerned with understanding and classifying the objects in an environment.

- Exploration, which is concerned with finding out about a local environment and how that environment relates to other environments.

- Wayfinding, which is concerned with navigating toward a known destination.

Exploration focuses on understanding what objects exist in an environment and how the objects are related. Object identification is concerned with finding out information about the objects. Exploration will enable people to find categories and clusters of objects and how they spread across environments. Exploration is concerned with finding interesting configurations of objects and understanding the spatial relations between them such as distance, direction, density and order.

Navigation is concerned with both the location of things and with what those things mean for an individual. For example, you might be given some driving instructions to get to your friend's house that includes "turn left at the grocer's shop, you can't miss it," only to drive straight past the supposedly obvious landmark. Objects in an environment have different meanings and are more or less important for different people.

A lot of work in psychology has been done on how people learn about environments and with the development of "cognitive maps"; the mental representations that people are assumed to have of their environment. In particular Barbara Tversky has explored the issues in great detail (e.g., Tversky, 2003). She discusses how people's representations of spaces are rarely wholly complete or static. They will involve bits of memories, stories, encounters with the environment and the perspective from which they are considering the space. Ecological considerations are concerned with the cues that people draw from the immediate environment as they interact with it. People develop knowledge of the space over time and through the experience of interacting with and within a space.

Recall from Chapter 2 the discussion about how much knowledge is "in the head" and how much is "in the world." There are many objects in the world that hold information for people (i.e., information artifacts, Section 5.2) to help them navigate. Signposts are an obvious example that show direction, distance and names of locations. Maps are another example, though of course different maps show different objects in the environment (try looking at Google maps and Apple maps for your local environment and see the differences).

Besides the activities of exploration and object identification, people will engage in wayfinding. Wayfinding is concerned with how people work out how to reach their destination. For

Downs and Stea (1973) and Passini (1992) the process involves four steps: orienting oneself in the environment, choosing the correct route, monitoring this route, and recognizing that the destination has been reached. To do this people use a variety of aids such as signposts, maps and guides. They exploit landmarks in order to have something to aim for. They use "dead reckoning" at sea or elsewhere when there are no landmarks. With dead reckoning you calculate your position by noting the direction you have headed, the speed of travel and the time that has passed. This is usually correlated with a landmark whenever possible.

Learning to find ones way in a new space is another aspect of navigation considered by psychologists. First, we learn a linked list of items. Then we get to know some landmarks and can start relating our position with regard to these landmarks. We learn the relative position of landmarks and start building mental maps of parts of the space in between these landmarks. These maps are not all complete. Some of the "pages" are detailed, others are not, and more importantly, the relation between the pages are not perfect. Some may be distorted with respect to one another.

Psychologists also distinguish three different types of knowledge that people have of an environment: landmark, route and survey knowledge (Downs and Stea, 1973). Landmark knowledge is the simplest sort of spatial knowledge in which people just recognize important features of the environment. Gradually they will fill in the details between landmarks and form route knowledge. As they become more familiar with the environment they will develop survey knowledge, the "cognitive map" of the environment.

The essential thing about designing for navigation is to keep in mind the different activities that people undertake in a space—object identification, wayfinding and exploration—and the different purposes and meanings that people will bring to the space. Of course designing for navigation has been the concern of architecture, interior design and urban planning for years and many useful principles have been developed. For example, the principals of universal design (see http://idea.ap.buffalo.edu/udny/Section4-1c.htm) as applied to wayfinding discuss how to design paths so that people do not get lost, how to design markers (natural or fabricated features of the environment), how to identify nodes, links and districts using the structure identified by Kevin Lynch as discussed in Chapter 3 (Lynch, 1960).

The practical aim of navigation design is to encourage people to develop a good understanding of the space in terms of landmark, route and survey knowledge. However, another aim is to create spaces that are enjoyable, engaging and involving. Design (as ever) is about form and function and how these can be harmoniously united. We saw in Chapter 3 how Norberg-Schulz (1980) discussed the character of spaces and the aesthetics of environments. These all have an impact on navigation. Too much similarity between different areas of an environment can cause confusion. The design should encourage people to recognize and recall an environment, to understand the context and use of the environment and to map the functional to the physical form of the space. Another important design principle from architecture is the idea that people gain a gradual knowledge of the space through use. Designers should aim for a "responsive environment," ensuring the availability of alternative routes, the legibility of landmarks, paths and districts and the ability to undertake a range of activities. Gordon Cullen was an architect who focused on the gradual unfolding nature of vistas as one walked through an environment. His ideas of "serial vision" led him to develop the sense of "hereness" and "thereness," making people aware of where they were going and making the environment legible so that they find their way and enjoy the experience (Cullen, 1964).

8.1.1   SIGNS

Good, clear signposting of spaces is critical in the design of spaces. There are three primary types of sign that designers can use. Informational signs provide information on objects, people and activities and hence aid object identification and classification. Directional signs provide route and survey information and often distance information. Directional signs often use sign hierarchies. One type of sign will provide general directions at a global scale, indicating the main areas of interest (such as major cities in a road network), along with other signs that provide local directions and local information. Warning and reassurance signs provide feedback or information on actual or potential actions within the environment and naming of places so people know when they have reached their destination.

Of course any particular sign may serve more than one purpose and an effective signage system will not only help people in getting to their desired destination, it will also make them aware of alternative options. Signage needs to integrate with the environment in which it is situated aesthetically so that it will help both good and poor navigators. Consistency of signage is important, but so is being able to distinguish different types of sign.

8.1.2   MAPS AND GUIDES

Maps are a central navigational technology. There are many different sorts of map from the very detailed and realistic to the highly abstract schematic. Schematic maps such as the map of the London underground, or New York subway show logical relationships between stations, but do not show the geographical relationships. "You are here" (YAH) maps are important for orientating oneself to an environment. Route maps do not provide the birds-eye view that most maps provide, but instead show paths through the environment.

Maps are social things—they are there to provide information and help people explore, understand and find their way through spaces. They should be designed to fit in with the signage system. Like signs there will often be a need for maps at different levels of abstraction. A global map that shows the whole extent of the environment will need to be supplemented by local maps showing the details of what is nearby.

Modern-day maps on smartphones, satnavs and tablets can make use of the GPS system to locate the individual and use addresses to find a destination. They can plan different routes depending on settings—the "pretty route," the shortest or the quickest—and they highlight different objects in the environment. As we see in the next chapter these locative media offer opportunities for new experiences.

Guidebooks provide another view of environments and can be oriented to providing information for different types of activity. Those interested in history can have a historical guide and those interested in wildlife can have a different guide. Guides and guidebooks provide much more detail about the objects in the space than they do about the spatial relationships. In this respect they support wayfinding and object identification, but do not support exploration to the same extent as maps do.

8.1.3   SOCIAL NAVIGATION

A well-designed environment with good signage and well-designed navigational aids such as maps will be conducive to good navigation, but even in the best-designed environment people will often turn to other people for information on navigation rather than use more formalized information artifacts (Section 5.1). When navigating cities people often ask other people for advice rather than study maps. Information from other people is usually personalized and adapted to suit the individual's needs. A short conversation to confirm what a person knows and what they do not know can ensure that navigational information is tailored to the individual and their interests. Even when we are not directly looking for information we use a wide range of cues, both from features of the environment and from the behavior of other people, to manage our activities. We might be influenced to follow a path because it seems well trodden, we walk into a sunny courtyard because it looks attractive or we go to see what is happening if we see a crowd gathered. We find our way through spaces by talking to or following the trails of others. This whole myriad of uses that people make of other people—whether directly or indirectly—we call social navigation (Höök et al., 2003).

8.2   NAVIGATION IN INFORMATION SPACE

In digital and information spaces, people still have to find their way through them, but the physics are different. Indeed some people would consider navigation of information and digital spaces to be quite different from navigation in geographical spaces as there is no body to be moved. However, we treat them as essentially similar activities, with the main difference being that the navigators in digital space have to move without the full range of sensory inputs of a physical body. The key thing for us is that design principles transfer from geographic to information spaces.

As we saw in Chapter 5, information spaces include both interactive and non-interactive devices and systems. In information spaces people face similar problems and undertake similar activities as they do in geographical spaces. They may be engaged in wayfinding—searching for a known piece of information. They may be engaged in exploration of the space to see what information is there or they may be engaged in object identification—understanding details about the objects in a space. They will move rapidly between these activities and they will pick up new information from the local environment. People will rely on designers putting information in an environment to remind them of different functions and options that are available. Information spaces can be seen as having different districts, with nodes and paths linking the sections together. Landmarks will help people to recognize where they are in a space and hopefully help them to plan and monitor a route to where they want to go. People will have simple route knowledge of some information spaces and survey knowledge of others.

For example a graphical user interface to an application such as Apple's Keynote has menu headers across the top indicating the main districts of functions. Click on one of these and you are given details of the local areas. Open up an "inspector" window and you will find information about objects. There is a clear sense of distance between parts of an information space such as an application as measured by the number of clicks, scrolls and double clicks that are required to get from editing a file, say, to formatting the paragraph.

Smartphone apps typically describe much smaller spaces than desktop applications and this makes navigation through an app more manageable. They provide menus to cluster objects into categories and then swipes to scroll down a list. The main districts of "favorites," "recents" and "contacts" are listed along the bottom of an address book app and it takes four taps to find my way to recent missed calls.

The design of navigation mechanisms is the second main pillar of information architecture for web design (Garrett, 2010). Overall guidelines for web design focus on providing navigational support through good labeling so that the meaning of the objects and areas is clear. A good menu structure—both the global menu that is typically along the top of a page, and the local menu that is typically on the left hand side—and good use of metadata will support navigation.

Navigation bars—both local and global—are essentially signposts and landmarks, leaving the site visitor to pick their way through the site structure. Site maps and good feedback on where people are in the structure will also help people navigate a website. Another alternative is to provide a clear path through a part of the site. This is particularly important when a number of activities or pages have to be visited in sequence. A site "wizard" can help here that guides people and explains what each activity is for. Often this is simply a succession of pages, such as when buying a ticket or booking a flight.

One of the significant features of an information space that distinguishes it from a physical space is searching. Search engines change the way people navigate, because they no longer have to follow the information architecture to get from one place to another. The analogy in geographical space is when you leap into a taxi and say the name of your destination. You do not have to worry about the physical architecture in order to get there. The provision of metadata is essential for effective searching of information spaces, but so is knowing exactly what sort of documents the search engine is searching. For example, is the content of different documents searched, or is it just the web pages themselves? Does it include PDF files, or Word files in which case is it the whole content or just some tagged key words? Sites should indicate what is searched and provide options to search different types of content. Even with searching, if the search result retrieves more than one object then the user is back to navigating through a list by scrolling (exploration) and clicking on items to find out exactly what they are (object identification).

Recall from Chapter 5 that the design of the information architecture is critical to the UX of navigating an information space. With a fine-grained ontology for the architecture, navigation becomes mostly moving between objects. With a coarse-grained architecture navigation is concerned with moving within objects. Moving between objects means that there has to be a sequence with items in "before" and "after" spatial relationships (e.g., objects in a list). The user can often change the attribute that is used to order the list, but you will still have a list. Moving within an object typically requires some form of scrolling, or labeling that supports hyperlinking. Designers need to think about the input devices that there are on different devices to support these different types of navigation.

8.2.1 NAVIGATION IN VIRTUAL ENVIRONMENTS

In VEs navigation is typically quite different from other information spaces. Users can "fly over" areas of the environment and zoom down into particular districts. They can then virtually walk around and inspect the objects that are there. They can leap across the environment using hyperlinks and use search functions. The navigational mechanisms in something like Second Life are very complex. In many games, players have to control their avatar to get from one location to another and maps are often included as part of the navigational features so that the player has both a first-person view on the main screen and an allocentric view of the space in the top corner. Many novel visualizations (Card, 2012) make use of these zooming and fly-over techniques.

8.3   SOCIAL NAVIGATION OF INFORMATION SPACE

Social navigation of information space encompasses a whole collection of techniques and designs that make people aware of others and of what others have done and make people aware of other people. Increasingly social media are integrated with information spaces to allow and enable methods of social navigation. For example it may be more effective to put out a message on Twitter asking for a recommendation for a good restaurant than it is to search a website. Knowing about communities and groups and their interests brings a different perspective on navigating the sometimes-soulless information spaces. Locative media can be very effective in providing social navigation. Thanks to the advances in positioning technologies an electronic message can be left associated with a particular place. When another person (suitably technologically equipped) arrives at the place the system alerts him or her to the message.

Filtering mechanisms can be used to make information spaces smaller and more navigable. In many apps, people can choose which aspects of the information space they are interested in, or can select particular channels of information. For example, in the whole information space of the weather forecast, we usually select our local area to display on our smartphone. In a smartphone guide to a city I might select history and literature as the two channels of information that I am interested in.

Recommender systems make suggestions to people for information based on what other people with similar tastes like or dislike. Personal profiles are matched and the system creates clusters of users with similar tastes. Book recommendations from the Amazon sites are probably the best examples of a mature recommender system. People who subscribe to Amazon can have the system recommend books based on those that they have bought previously and on those that they rank.

Another method of providing social navigation is to provide a tag (or "hash tag," or metadata) so that whenever a user comes upon a new piece of information she can see what other people with similar interests as her think of that particular piece of information. Some sort of rating of the information objects have to be done by the users of the system so the system can create and cluster personal profiles. Ratings can be done either explicitly and/or implicitly. Travel sites such as TripAdvisor use this way of collecting social media about locations that help others navigate.

Readware uses the trails of what other people have done in the past to tell people something about how to navigate the information space. The familiar technique to automatically change the colors on the links in a web page when a person has visited that page reminds us that we have already been to that part of the space. Icons can be used to show the density of visits or number of sites that are in a part of the space.

Social navigation uses social media (Section 7.2) to support the activities that people undertake in information spaces. Through general principles of awareness of others, and particularly awareness of other people who are similar to us in some way, through allowing people to share things easily and to quickly and effectively exchange short messages (such as press "like") the social becomes a critical part of information navigation.

8.4   SUMMARY

Moving through and understanding spaces is an important human activity. Navigation in information spaces is a feature of our modern technologically enabled world. We can learn much from studying navigation in geographical spaces and apply design principles from urban planning and architecture. The principles of how people find their way in information spaces are the same as those in geographical spaces. The differences are that people have far less sensory cues in information spaces (the lack of social signals, see Section 7.1). Also in information spaces the physics are different—people can jump to different parts of the space, fly over data landscapes and move through virtual walls. In information spaces, design is even more important.

People move through environments as they undertake their activities. They will move through both the physical space and through the information space (the semiotic space) that sits alongside it. They move between object identification, wayfinding and exploration. The design of both physical and information spaces rely on principles of legibility of the space allowing people to gain route and survey knowledge.

CHAPTER 9

Blended Spaces

Interaction designers frequently find themselves designing not simply some device or service, but also a physical environment. They might be designing a new meeting room or developing a foyer area in a building that has a number of large linked screens that provide various services. On another occasion, designers will find themselves designing some locative media such as a location-based tourist app. Rather than just bolting a digital space on top of a physical space, designers need to consider how the different spaces fit together and what the conceptual and social spaces are like.

Blended spaces are spaces where a physical space is deliberately integrated in a close-knit way with a digital space. Blended spaces go beyond mixed reality (Milgram and Kishino, 1994) and conceptually are much closer to tangible interactions (Ishii and Ullmer, 1997) where the physical and digital are completely coupled. The aim of blended space design is to enable people to feel present in a blended space, acting directly on the content of the blended space (cf. Section 2.5 on presence).

In Chapter 6 we introduced the concept of blending, the creative process of bringing together concepts from different spaces in order to create a new space, with its own emergent properties. Here we apply the ideas of conceptual blending to both physical and digital spaces to create new blended spaces of interaction. We also see how the work on semiotics in Chapter 2 and information artifacts discussed in Chapter 5 come together to show how we can navigate blended spaces.

9.1 BLENDED INTERACTION

O'Hara et al. (2011) refer to the distributed spaces linked by very high-quality video-conferencing systems such as Halo as blended spaces because of the apparently seamless joining of remote physical locations. In systems such as Halo, great attention is paid to the design of the physical conference rooms and to the angle and geometry of the video technologies in order to give the impression that two distant rooms are collocated. High-end video conferencing supports the collaborative activity of business discussions, but it does not deal well with shared information resources. O'Hara, et al. (2011) use the term "blended interaction spaces" for "blended spaces in which the interactive groupware is incorporated in ways spatially consistent with the physical geometries of the video-mediated set-up." Their paper explores the design of a blended interaction space that highlights the importance of the design of the physical space in terms of human spaces and the different proxemics (Hall, 1969) of personal spaces, intimate spaces and so on.

Jetter et al. (2012) also discuss blended interaction. They develop a framework for looking at the personal, social, workflow and collaborative aspects of blended interaction. Benyon and Mival (2014) describe the design of their interactive collaborative environment (ICE, discussed later in this chapter) focusing on the close integration of hardware, software and room design to create new interactive spaces for creativity.

In addition to these examples of blended spaces and interaction in room environments, the idea of blended spaces has been applied to the domain of digital tourism. Here the emphasis is on providing appropriate digital content at appropriate physical places in order to provide a good UX for tourists. The concept of blending has also been used for the design of ambient assisted living environments for older people (Hoshi et al., 2011) and for the design of products including a blood taking machine (Markussen, 2009) and a table lamp.

In our treatment of physical spaces (Chapter 3), digital spaces (Chapter 4) and information spaces we identified four key characteristics for describing spaces: ontology, topology, volatility and agency. The ontology of the spaces concerns the objects in the spaces, how many they are, how big they are, how they are distributed and what functions and facilities they have. In physical space the objects are the locations, nodes, districts and so on. In the digital space they are the information artifacts, the devices and the software. The topology of the spaces concerns how those objects are related to one another. There are distance and direction relations, clusters and categories of objects. The spread and density of the objects determine the topology. The dynamics or volatility of the spaces concerns how the objects and elements in the spaces move and change over time. The agency in the spaces concerns the people in the spaces, the artificial agents and the opportunities for action in the spaces.

Recall that in conceptual blending (Section 6.3) two input spaces are perceived to have some common attributes that arise from a more generic space. These input spaces are projected into a blended space where some or all of the common structure is preserved, but where the blending of the input spaces results in a new space with new properties. By understanding the correspondences between the physical and the digital spaces—in terms of the ontology, topology, volatility and agency of those spaces—designers will produce new blended spaces that have emergent properties. In these spaces, people will not be in a physical space with some digital content bolted on. People will be present in a blended space and this will give rise to new experiences and new ways of engaging with the world.

The conceptualization of blended spaces illustrated in Figure 9.1. The job of the designer is to bring the spaces together in a natural, intuitive way to create a good user experience. The designer should design the blended space according to the principles of designing with blends (Imaz and Benyon, 2007; see also Section 6.3) such as drawing out the correspondences between the topology of the physical and digital spaces, using the integration principle to deliver a whole experience and designing at a human scale.

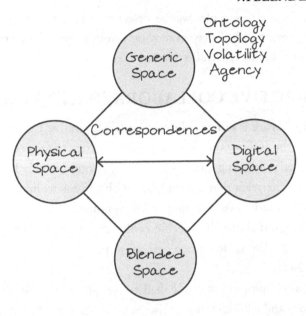

Figure 9.1: Conceptual blending in mixed reality spaces.

Another consideration that is important in the design of blended spaces is that the physical and the digital spaces rarely co-exist. There are anchors, or touch points, where the physical is linked to the digital, but there are many places where the physical and the digital remain separate. QR codes or GPS are examples of anchor technologies that bring the physical and the digital together. In blended spaces, people move between the physical, the digital and the blended spaces. This movement through and between spaces is an important part of the blended space concept and leads on to issues of navigation in blended spaces.

The blended space encompasses a conceptual space of understanding and making meaning and this is where the principles of designing with blends are so important. People need to be aware of both the physical and the digital spaces, what they contain, and how they are linked together. People need to understand the opportunities afforded by the blended space and to be able to unpack the blend to see how and why the spaces are blended in a particular way. People need to be aware of the structure of the physical and the digital, so that there is a harmony: the correspondences between the objects in the spaces. The overall aim of blended spaces is to design for a great UX, at a human scale.

Although they do not use the term "blended spaces" Ina Wagner and her colleagues provide a number of examples of mixed reality experiences that aim to bring together physical and digital spaces (Wagner et al., 2009). They explore many of the issues that we have raised in this book, from users of their augmented reality maps trying to establish a common ground (Section 6.1) to the social aspects of physical interaction (Chapter 7), to tangible interaction in the context of device ecologies (Section 4.2). In their examples we see designers trying to create a sense of presence in the mixed reality environment and of players moving through the hybrid trajectories discussed by Benford et al. (Benford et al., 2011; see also Section 7.3).

9.2   AN INTERACTIVE COLLABORATIVE ENVIRONMENT (ICE)

One example of a blended space is our own Interactive Collaborative Environment (ICE). The aim of the project to develop the ICE was to provide a great experience for people and to give them an insight on what leading edge meeting spaces can be like. A number of whole room environments have been developed over the years that are equipped with various technological devices and combinations of interactive white boards and projection equipment. Each of these raises important issues about collaboration and about the specific configuration of surfaces and devices that were configured. We do not intend to review these here as, to prefigure our conclusions, each ICE has its own specific design issues.

As with all real-world projects, the ICE had to comply with a number of constraints such as the existence of a room and a budget. It was also to be a "bring your own device" (BYOD) environment. The philosophy underlying the design focused on providing an environment that would help people within it fulfill their activities and do so in pleasurable intuitive ways. Wherever possible the aim is to remove function from the content of devices (screens, laptops, mobile devices) and instead consider these devices as portals onto function and content that is resident in a shared space. This should enable and facilitate real time, concurrent, remote collaboration. Another key aim is to enable the seamless mixing of digital and analogue media. People bring notebooks, pens and paper to meetings and we are keen that such analogue media should co-exist happily alongside the digital spaces.

9.2.1   THE PHYSICAL SPACE

The physical space that was available for the ICE was an empty office, so the design started with a room, a vision and a budget of €150,000 about a third of which went on technologies for the digital space, a third on room alterations and a third on necessary infrastructure. After extensive research into the options available we settled on the following technologies. A 46" n-point HD (1080p) multi-touch LCD screen mounted on the end wall of the room. This screen uses the diffused illumination (DI) method for detecting multi-touch and is capable of detecting finger and hand orientation as well as distinguishing between different users' hands. A 108" n-point multi-touch rear projection boardroom table, also using DI, is the centerpiece of the room. The table can recognize and interact with objects placed on its surface such as mobile phones, laptops or books using infrared fiducial markers.

The table was designed specifically for the space available, which determined its dimensions and technical specification. Due to the requirement of using the table both when sitting and stand-

ing the surface is 900mm from the floor, the standard ergonomic height for worktops. Four 42"
HD (1080p) dual point multi-touch LCD screens utilizing infrared overlays are mounted on the
room's side walls. Each screen is driven by a dedicated Apple Mac Pro, which can triple boot into
Mac OSX, Windows 7 and Linux. The room has 8-channel wireless audio recording for 8 wearable
microphones as well as 2-channel recording for 2 room microphones. Each audio channel can be
sent individually to any chosen destination (either a computer in the ICE or to an external storage
via IP) or combined into a single audio stream. A webcam allows for high definition video (1080p)
to be recorded locally or streamed over IP. The recording facility is used both as a means of archiving
meetings (for example, each audio channel can record an individual participant) or for tele- and
video-conferencing activities. Any recordings made can be stored both locally and on an external
cloud storage facility for remote access.

The walls are augmented with the Mimio™ system to serve as digital whiteboards, thus
when something is written on the whiteboard it is automatically digitally captured. Importantly no
application needs to be launched before capture begins; the process of contact between the pen and
the wall initiates the digital capture.

9.2.2 THE DIGITAL SPACE

The ICE hardware has been selected to offer the widest range of development and design opportunities and as such we have remained platform agnostic. To achieve this, all the hardware runs on
multiple operating systems (Mac OS X, Windows 7 and 8, Linux). Alongside the standard development environments are the emerging options for multi-touch, central to which is the Tangible
User Interface Objects (TUIO) protocol, an open framework that defines a common protocol and
API for tangible multi-touch surfaces. TUIO enables the transmission of an abstract description
of interactive surfaces, touch events and tangible object states from a tracker application and sends
it to a client application. All the hardware in the room is TUIO compliant. The TUIO streams
generated by the screens and table in the ICE are passed to the computers via IP thus enabling the
possibility for more extensive remote screen sharing. Indeed, if a remote participant has the capacity
to generate a TUIO stream of their own, as is the capability with many modern laptop track-pads,
they can collaborate with the ICE surfaces both through traditional point and click methods but
also multi-touch gestures.

A key design issue for the software is that there is no complex software architecture required.
All applications are available at the top level; the TUIO protocol means that any device running it
can interact with other devices running it. This allows for easy integration of mobile devices into the
room and sharing control across devices. Since everything in the room is interconnected through
the Internet, the room demonstrates how such sharing of content and manipulation of content
could be physically distributed.

In terms of software, the ICE makes extensive use of freely available applications such as Evernote™, Skype™, etc. A key design decision for the ICE is to keep it simple and leverage the power of robust third-party services. People need to be able to come into the room and understand it and to conceptualize the opportunities it offers for new ways of working. It is little use having applications buried away in a hierarchical menu system where they will not be found. Hence the design approach is to make the applications all available at the top level. One particularly important application is Dropbox™, which is used to enable the sharing of content across devices. Since the Dropbox™ service is available across most devices, any content put into one device is almost immediately available on another. For example, take a photo on an iPhone or Android Phone and it is immediately available on the table and wall screens. Essentially Dropbox™ works as the synching bridge across all the separate computers driving each surface, which enables a seamless "shared repository" experience for users. Any file they utilize on one surface is also available on any other, as well as remotely should the user have the appropriate access authority.

9.2.3   THE CONCEPTUAL SPACE

The conceptual space concerns how people understand what the novel blend of physical and digital spaces allows them to do and how they frame their activities in the context of that understanding. There are a lot of novel concepts to be understood. For example, people need to understand that the screens on the walls are not computers, but are windows onto data content in the cloud. They will recognize the Internet Explorer icon on a screen and rightly conceptualize that this gives them Internet access, but they may not realize that they can save files to a shared Dropbox™ folder and hence enable files to be viewed through different screens. They need to conceptualize the wall screens as input and output zones that can show different views at different times. People who have used the ICE a few times come to understand that they can see an overview of some data set on one screen and the detail on another and that this is useful for particular activities. The wall screens can be easily configured to mirror each other, or to show separate content. The challenge for spaces such as the ICE is that people do not have a mental model, a conceptualization, of the space when they first arrive. It is up to the designers to present an informative, coherent image of the system that enables people to develop an appropriate conceptual understanding of the opportunities. For example we developed a control room map to help people conceptualize the interaction between the different screens and how any screen could be the source of an image displayed on any number of other screens. This is one example of an attempt to provide a way into the conceptual space. Restricting the functionality of the digital space and providing this through a few familiar icons is another.

9.2.4   THE BLENDED SPACE

We can summarize the ICE through the lens of conceptual blending as illustrated in Figure 9.2. The ontology of the space simply defines the walls, windows, tables and chairs, blended with the screens on the walls, interactive table and interactive whiteboards. Part of the topology projected into the blended space is the way that difference screens can be configured to mirror each other or to display different content. The volatility of the space does cause problems as different groups of people configure the room differently and others do not know how to reconfigure it for their own needs. We have recognized that the design of the blended space should have included a large "reset" button, so that people can conceptualize how to get things back to the normal setting. The room supports agency in that it lets people move around and form collaborative groupings easily and effectively.

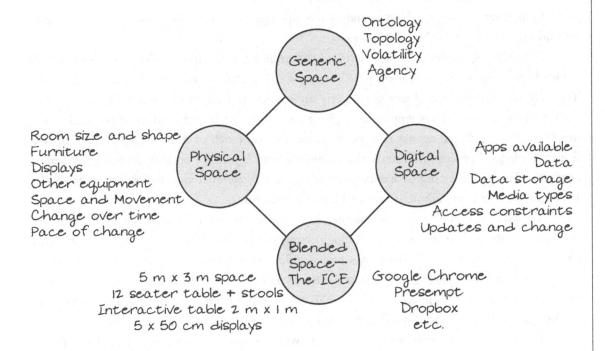

Figure 9.2: The ICE as a blended space.

9.3   DIGITAL TOURISM AS A BLENDED SPACE

The key features of the ontology of tourist attractions are the high-level points of interest (POIs). A location might be the natural wonders of a national park such as Yellowstone, or Mount Rushmore. A location could be a series of buildings in a historic neighborhood, grave plots in a cemetery or a great open field. A location could have a series of temporary interrelated events such as Civil War reenactments in Gettysburg, PA. Although the reenactment of the Battle of Gettysburg could be considered a main attraction, designers of a blended experience need to consider POIs on both Confederate and Union base camps, before, during and after the great battle. Although outlying activities may not be the main event, understanding and integrating side events is important. Furthermore, tourists also need to know about location utilities such as bathrooms, bus stops, eateries, gift shops, etc. Designers need to be aware of the ontology of a location's activities and POIs on several granular levels.

The physical topology describes how different POIs are related at a given tourist location. The relationships between POIs derive from the constraints of physical environments, tours, educational programs and various levels of personal preferences and interests. A tourist location might cover many hundreds of acres with few other people around. Other locations may have many POIs packed into a very small area. Understanding the topology of a tourist location is key to developing novel design solutions for blended spaces.

Agents in the digital space are another key feature affecting the usability and enjoyment of a blended space. Agency describes the possible ways a visitor might interact with and within a space. Typically, national parks and tourist sites rely on wayside signage to interface with their visitors. Park rangers are sometimes employed to give tours. However, in the context of blended spaces, properly utilizing digital agency is imperative. Having too much or too little agency can distract from the physical spaces or frustrate the visitor. Depending on the ontology, topology, historical context and user profiles, digital agency could be a guided directional tour leading visitors to specific POIs, an unguided serendipitous tour or a blend of the two.

The volatility of the space is another key consideration for blended spaces. Objects and people move through spaces and the topology changes over time. Spaces may change on a regular basis such as daily or seasonally or owing to specific events. Other spaces are much less volatile. Each season may bring new attractions to a national park. A tourist destination may have skiing in the winter, rafting in the spring, camping in the summer, and hayrides in the fall. Tourist locations might change daily, going from a family-friendly environment to a raucous nightlife.

Designers need to be cognizant of how and why the ontology, topology, agency and volatility interrelate under the context of the historical content coupled with personal interests. Understanding these relationships is key because it begins to build the framework to how and why digital spaces blend with physical spaces to create the UX.

9.3.1   A POETRY GARDEN

One example of a blended tourist space was the development of a poetry garden in St. Andrew Square in Edinburgh, UK, a public park in the center of the city. We were commissioned by the Unesco Edinburgh City of Literature to come up with suggestions for how to turn this into a poetry garden. Our first activity was to try to understand the physical space and how it was used, so we undertook several hours of observation at different times of day. In order to develop the broad brief of "create a poetry garden" we undertook a number of brainstorming sessions and interviews with people who use the space. A presentation of the idea of creating a poetry garden was followed by two focus groups of local residents. As a result of this data gathering we developed the concept for the garden. This led to the development of a digital space, and augmentations of the physical space that would be blended in a harmonious way to suit the needs of tourists and local people using the park on a regular basis.

The Physical Space

St. Andrew Square is used in a number of different ways. It is a crossing between shops on the northeast and the southwest sides. It is a space where people sit and rest, eat lunch or play with their children. There are several areas sheltered by trees and other open grass areas. The square has a café toward the northeast corner and an attractive garden and pond around the tall central statue of a local dignitary. Throughout the year, different city events such as the book festival or science festival use this square as a showroom. The space is a highly dynamic or volatile area. Many people walk through the square on their way to work or between shops. Others bring their lunch to the space, or sit with family and friends to enjoy a break for the city traffic. The coffee shop is another center of interest. People, especially during the day are using this shop as a natural stopping point.

The Conceptual Space

Developing the concept of a poetry garden in this setting required us to consider the range of people who would be visiting it. The space needed to serve people who walked through the garden regularly, tourists and those who frequented more rarely. It was to serve the needs of those having a quick lunch and those who had more time sit at length. There was also an important consideration as to whether people would simply consume the content or whether they could contribute their own poems, comments or other content to the garden.

The Digital Space

The digital space involves both the hardware and software necessary to provide the services developed in the concept design. The technology we used in this design included speakers, projectors, QR codes, AR projections, GPS, mobile devices and private network systems. The content was of course, poetry, and there was much discussion about what sort of poetry was most appropriate for which purposes. Although the content of the actual poems was left open we delivered a number of designs that would produce the blended experience that would suit the brief.

The Blended Space

Overall the aim was to create a harmonious blend of the physical and the digital spaces to deliver a new UX and hence develop the garden into a blended space. The physical ontology of the different locations would drive the design of having different types of experience in different locations within the garden. The physical topology would drive the navigational aids to allow people to move between the locations and objects. In terms of the volatility of the space some experiences would suit people on the move and others for people relaxing for a longer time. Volatility was also important to the content of the digital space by changing the poems available in different places. With respect to the agency in the space, characters were introduced in the digital space to read poems.

This resulted in a number of concepts that, taken as a whole, would provide the blended space experience that we were looking for. The concepts that were delivered to the client included the following.

Carry a Poem. With this idea, digital poems would be created, embedded in QR codes and printed on napkins and cups at the coffee shop and in booklets that people could take away with them. This allowed people to take something physical away with them so that people would have something physical to remind them of their visit; the digital experience persists after the journey. Scanning the codes in the garden would create a social experience for visitors and returning to them later would enable them to keep in touch with the changing content.

Sound Showers. This idea involves a bench and localized speakers to create a serendipitous poem experience. Motion sensors would detect the user sitting down, therefore using more volume on the speakers. From the user's perspective, resting and enjoying a poem is a simultaneous action. Here the natural topology of the areas with trees led to the digital augmentation that did not require the user to have any other technology with them.

Project a Poet. This idea involved augmenting the existing seating areas with fiducial markers etched into the stone. Scanning these would enable an augmented reality experience delivered on a phone or tablet of a poet reading a poem. The additional narrative and character that this brings to the overall experience was intended to add to the agency of the space.

The 3D QR sculpture. This concept involved creating a large sculpture in the garden acting as both a physical and digital augmentation. This sculpture could be used as a QR code when the visitor was in the correct alignment. It would take the visitor to a web page where poems were displayed.

Summary

The design of the poetry garden aimed to create a blended space, bringing the digital space of the poetry content into the physical space of the garden and augmenting the physical space with other objects to deliver a harmonized UX for all the different users of the park. The AR projection fitted into the stone seats near the pond, the sound showers went into the sheltered areas, the sculpture on the main grassy area, carry a poem used QR codes and these were located near the entrances to the park. The design accommodated the volatile nature of the space through natural and rapid methods of access to the content, and the QR sculpture added collaboration between people as they tried to line up a QR reader with the sculpture as it would only act as a QR code from a certain angle.

The integration principle of conceptual blending was particularly important here, as we wanted people to see the garden as a whole and to enjoy the way the digital portals were distributed across the space. These portals were vital as they provide the transitions between the physical and digital spaces allowing people to navigate through both the digital and physical spaces.

9.3.2 THE VILLAGE MUSEUM

This case study illustrates the use of the blended space structure—the ontology, topology, volatility and agency—to discuss the design of an enhanced visitor experience at a living history museum (O'Keefe et al., 2014). The physical space was a large museum covering several hectares and dealing with life in America through the 17th, 18th and 19th centuries. Original buildings have been relocated to the museum and provide an engaging experience for visitors of all ages. Our brief was to design a blended space making use of the smart phones now carried by many people.

Ontology

The ontology of the physical space consists of the main POIs and the historical districts. The museum is large with many different locations. There are many historical buildings to visit across three centuries of historical villages and content. There are three explicit areas of the museum: pioneer, colonial and Victorian villages. Tourists can spend an entire week at the museum and not discover all there is to experience. Our design approach allows the visitor to select their path at the entrance of the park (an 18th-century tollbooth). We used the physical ontology of the existing museum infrastructure as a conceptual model of our digital service and storytelling architectures. At the tollbooth the digital ontology of the system allows the visitor to choose his/her own path. Once a visitor selects a village to explore they are greeted by an artificial agent in this case a video of one of the characters.

Agency

Currently, each village has staged physical agents or actors. Actors take on the persona of an 18th-century tinsmith or a lady of the 19th century. Interaction with the actors enables the visitors to ask questions and listen to stories about the actor's responsibilities and role in the society. Our design approach exploited the actor paradigm, not to simply replace existing human agents, but to develop new stories and new experiences for the visitor. In building the conceptual space we leveraged possible stories of the day to enable the visitor to participate in 17th, 18th or 19th-century social activities. Thus the design included video of actors playing out parts of the narrative that were triggered by a geo-fence at a particular POI.

Topology

Through digital agency visitors are invited to a Victorian wedding. The conceptual space of the wedding story creates a topological context or story for the visitor to follow. The storyline takes the visitor to pick up a gift from the tinsmith before the visitor and the digital agent go to the church. Once the gift is received they go to the church only to find the groom is missing. Searching for the groom, the visitor finds himself/herself running around the Victorian town in a frantic search for the groom, all the while, the visitor is learning about different Victorian buildings and social norms of the time. At the end of the story, the visitor finds the groom at the tavern. Everyone then returns to the church to participate in a blended Victorian wedding. As the visitor moves to POIs, taking photos and interacting between spaces, we use the location's content to generate souvenirs.

Volatility

The museum has activities all year round to attract new and seasonal visitors; hence we created a host of time period storylines to coincide with seasonal volatility. If the visiting tourist arrives in the summer and chooses the Victorian Village, the visitor will experience a Victorian Wedding. In contrast, the experience of arriving in December would be designed around the yuletide festivities of Christmas. Other than these changes to the digital content, to reflect the changing seasons, the overall structure of the experience is not subject to rapid change.

Summary

By understanding and leveraging the four key characteristics of blended spaces we aim to create enhanced user experiences. The new experiences that can be offered through linking digital content delivered through a phone to physical locations can be designed to take advantage of the blended space approach. The key thing is to look for the correspondences between the spaces in terms of ontology, topology, volatility and agency and to exploit these in the blended space UX.

9.4   NAVIGATION IN BLENDED SPACES

The concept of a blended space draws on the ideas of mixed reality, anchors that connect the physical and digital spaces and the multilayered nature of interaction in this medium. As we discussed in Chapter 8, people will navigate through spaces. For example in the Village museum the app included a compass that pointed to the location of the next POI. The poetry garden contained no signage, but instead the concepts were there to be explored and discovered. In this section we highlight the navigational issues of blended spaces by looking at two other examples.

9.4.1   NEON KNIGHTS

Neon Knights was an event that took place at a Digital Arts Festival in Dundee, November 2010. The designers were tasked to promote the festival via the means of a game that also advertised some of the festival sponsors. Their response was to produce a QR-driven "treasure hunt" that promoted the festival via posters that were located across the city. In the run up to the event the posters promoted the festival encouraging local people to take part. During the festival the posters became the key component in the game allowing participants to collect points for every QR code that was "captured" via a mobile device. The posters then had a dual role, to encourage local people to attend the festival "bringing them in" as well as encouraging participants at the festival to "get out" and experience Dundee. Additionally, each code was linked to a particular offer from a local business sponsor, e.g., two-for-one cinema tickets, 10% off a meal, etc., providing incentives to take part and linking local business into the festival.

The blend is illustrated in Figure 9.3. The main objects in the physical space (the ontology) are the posters and they are topologically related through their physical locations in different parts of the city. These provide the grounding for the anchor points into the digital space provided by the QR codes. In the digital space there are other objects concerning the collection of points and how these relate to the offers that are blended with the physical locations of the local businesses. The temporary nature of the event means that the experience is volatile and the sense of competition and drive adds to the dynamics of the blended space. The new agency provided by the blended space concerns the treasure hunt, the prizes and the special offers.

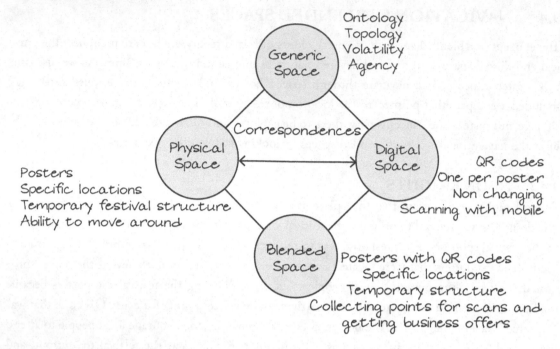

Figure 9.3: Blended space for Neon Knights.

In order to understand navigation in blended spaces we need to draw upon the understanding of navigation presented in Chapter 8 and on the medium of interaction that we discussed in Chapter 2. We can conceive of the space of the city as an object that is encountered bodily by the functional perception/action loops of the participant players. Players have to engage bodily with the city in order to move around and collect points, therefore embodied interaction is already taking place as part of the game and one can surmise that the embodied schemas for moving around this environment are involved in the sense-making process. Likewise, players must also marshal whatever general knowledge of cities they have in order to navigate through the city. People's knowledge of buildings, roads, paths, traffic and people would all be helpful for interpreting what they encounter, even though they may not be related to the specific features of Dundee.

The posters themselves are multifaceted information artifacts (Section 5.1) composed not only of locations but also of content in the form of advertising for the festival and QR codes for playing the game. The QR codes provide the anchor points through which to engage with the digital content. The advertising that accompanies provides the context for the game to be played.

Technologically, the mobile devices used to interact with the posters are another mediating mechanism. On one level the QR code-reading software very simply translates the QR code into the URL that points the browser to usable content. This is relatively trivial for the participant in that all they have to do is switch on the app and point the device at the QR code in order to read it. However, it is this physical/digital translation that really makes the game possible by binding the two spaces together. Scanning the physical bar code reveals content related to the game in the form of web pages that communicate the points scored. In the background these points are tallied up and an overall score for each participant is maintained until the game time is up. Content related to the operating system of the device is of course necessary to make this possible.

One interesting thing to note is that specific content in terms of knowledge about the location of posters must be an emergent feature of the game as these locations are unknown to begin with and finding these locations is key to scoring points. Thus semiotically, finding the locations of posters is an active interpretation of the city made possible through embodied interaction within the context of the game. Likewise, knowledge of gameplay must evolve and grow. Content related to game playing must initially be employed in terms of understanding the rules of the game. However, the experience of playing the game must increase knowledge of game playing in general, perhaps specifically introducing conceptual knowledge about QR Treasure hunts. All the while, another concept is forming in the minds of the participants, about the festival. The advertisements on the posters, the web content and the experience of moving around the city all combine together to establish new knowledge of what the festival is all about.

Our analysis reveals that even simple blending of physical, technological and cultural spaces leads to highly complex interwoven acts of signification and interpretation in the conceptual space. The city and the festival are different spaces that are layered one on top of the other to form a blended space. This layering is made possible by the manifestation of mediating elements that physically exist in the environment of the city (the posters and QR codes) that are accessed by participants acting in the world with their mobile phones (mediating devices) to reveal digital content (points). Interaction constantly moves between the ready-to-hand operations of moving across the city and operating the QR reading mobile device to capture the points and the present-at-hand activities of recognizing the posters, reading interface signs and planning routes across the city in order to maximize point gains within the allotted time.

9.4.2   LAST DAY IN EDINBURGH

"Last Day in Edinburgh" was a technology enhanced walk through the streets of that part of the city known as the "The Old Town." Based on the works of the famous writer Robert Louis Stevenson (RLS), particularly "Edinburgh, Picturesque Notes," the walk uses location-based technology, strategically placed throughout the Old Town, to deliver snippets of RLS's writing to the participants' mobile phones, while they are actually in the location that RLS is referring to over 130 years ago. In a sense the participants are following in RLS's footsteps on a guided tour around the part of Edinburgh that RLS was familiar with. As the Old Town has changed little since 1878, much of what he described is still there today.

Six different locations (POIs), featuring particular landmarks, over a 0.7-mile course were carefully pinpointed in relation to RLS's writing and a map was created to display them. Pictures of RLS were placed in these environments in order to anchor the digital content to the location. An additional four anchor points were added along the route between these locations to provide additional information about RLS, e.g., poetry, pictures and video. The aim of this additional content was to establish a link between all the locations and an awareness of the experience as a totality. The walk took about 15 minutes to complete plus the time the users spent on the experiencing the content that was provided. Thus the main objects in the physical and digital spaces correspond 1:1, the places as they are today and the places as they were 130 years ago, the views as they are today and the views as they were then. The topologies of the spaces correspond with each other again providing a natural mapping for the blended space.

The structure of the blend is illustrated in Figure 9.4. The ontology of the physical and digital spaces are dictated by the specific places that RLS wrote about and of course the physical topology of the space dictates the relationship between the places. The user has to climb the hills and walk through the wynds (narrow lanes) in order to get to the next place on the walk. The walk is a stable, non-volatile structure because it is based around the physical places. However, at different times of day there will be other people around and moving through, so the overall UX depends on the volatility of others. In terms of agency the blended space provides the new experience of engaging with RLS's works in their physical location.

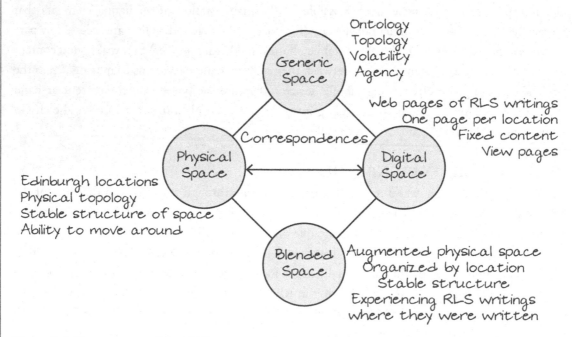

Figure 9.4: The structure of the RLS space.

Employing the same approach as outlined earlier, we can analyze the various components of the blended space to see how they combine together to allow for a meaningful experience to take place. Similar to the first example, the city (Old Town) can be considered as an object to be explored by the participants by bodily moving through the environment. We have the sights, sounds, smells and textures of Edinburgh itself. The quality of the light, the color and texture of the stone walls, the freshness and smell in the air are all facets of the real world that are available to the embodied participant present at the various locations visited. They were also available in a similar form to RLS when he was in Edinburgh, and at its core, it is this experience of the world that the participants are asked to compare with the mediated experience of RLS. Unlike the first example though, the participants are armed with a map that depicts a route that they must follow. The map is an information artifact that has it's own perceptible qualities but most importantly it is content of the tour's designer that is present on the map that defines the route to be taken and the locations in which to seek out the POIs.

In terms of embodied experience we have the participants' perceptual capabilities smoothly engaging with the environment in order to navigate the streets themselves. Successfully moving along the road, in the right direction, negotiating bends, curves, cars, cobles and curbs all require the use of embodied schemas in concert with content about cities in general to orchestrate sophisticated movement through a complex environment. Moreover, reading the map and perceiving the pictures of RLS at various points along the route plays an important part in being able to progress through the experience.

Embodied schemas lay the foundations for a reading of the material, we understand the orientation of the material, we understand the flow of the text, we perceive coherent wholes and parts in its structure and we begin to interpret what is seen. The device itself proceeds with its program of actions in order to render the digital content to the screen (or through the audio channel) making it available to the participant. This new congregation of signs feeds into the experience providing a new concept around RLS's words that describe the location as he saw it over 130 years ago. Participants interpret those words in relation to their location now.

9.5   SUMMARY

Blended spaces aim to bring the physical space together with the digital space to provide a new experience of blended interaction. By focusing on the ontology, topology, volatility and agency in the spaces, designers can develop the correspondences between the spaces in order to produce a suitable blend. The blended space will have its own properties that designers need to consider. The aim is to deliver a good UX in the blended space.

A key aspect of these new spaces is that people have to navigate them. In the context of an ICE-type environment people will be collaborating through some physical activity such as talking to each other, but then may access the digital space to bring up some media to illustrate what they are saying. The conversation may then continue with shared access to the digital content. In the context of digital tourism we may observe someone walking through a physical space, accessing some digital content on an iPad and then continuing his or her physical movement.

These different types of navigation can be illustrated with examples where we can see not just the physical movement but also the conceptualizations that people will have as they move through the conceptual and information spaces of understanding. In both RLS and the village there is additional layering of description and narrative content that provides a different way to engage with the environment that is not there when simply walking around on your own.

Blended spaces thus provide a new context for interaction design, bringing together the designer's knowledge of the design of physical spaces (Chapter 3), digital spaces (Chapter 4) and information spaces (Chapter 5) to create a new medium of interaction (Chapter 2). Designers need to focus on the whole UX, not on the technology and design for experience at a human scale.

CHAPTER 10

Places for Experience

We have now completed a tour around the different spaces of interaction that will make up the places for experience in the coming years. We have moved from space in Chapter 1 to place here in Chapter 10. The places of the future bring together the physical, digital, informational, blended, conceptual and social and some domain of activity—whether that is work, home, leisure or some hybrid system—to create a new medium, or rather new media, which people will inhabit. We can refer back to our notion of interaction as Pact. People are always engaged with some activities surrounded by, and interacting through, a medium of contexts and technologies. In the new places for experience we can expect to see a more nuanced blend of the physical and digital.

These new places are beginning to emerge, but they are very poorly designed at present. Even on holiday my wife and I now retire from the beach to a nearby bar and ask for beer, wine and the wi-fi password. I will read the online newspaper and check e-mail and we will talk about issues while googling to fill in the gaps of our knowledge. So here is a potential place for experience. It is often not a very good experience because the wi-fi is slow, the chairs are hard or the news is depressing. Indeed it might not get imbued with the notion of place at all if the physical location is not pleasant, or the social scene is not conducive to a post-beach convivial encounter and we will not return.

Typically in these situations, the information space has not been considered. How many such bars pay great attention to the lighting, the décor, the furniture, the planting, the music, the video, the service, the drinks and yet fail to pay attention to their information space? It seems to me the most obvious thing for a trendy bar to do is to create a blended space where the Internet access takes you not directly to Google and Outlook mail, but instead provides an overlaid information space that fits in with the ambience of the physical space they have spent so much effort designing. Surely such blended places will soon be a matter of course.

So, what do designers need to think about now to design for the places for experience of the next period? What will change in HCI and interaction design? And what does the next period bring?

10.1 INHABITING PLACES

The art of HCI will need to change if designers are to create experiences that allow people to feel present in and to move through, mixed reality blended places. HCI and interaction design have focused too much on interaction as a cognitive activity, on microinteractions and tasks, and not enough on providing great experiences through understanding how people form intentions, make meanings, have feelings and feel connected with their world.

Interaction design needs to address the aesthetics of UX in the design processes. Dewey (1934/2005), for example, distinguishes aesthetic experiences from other aspects of our life through placing it in between two extremes on a scale. On one end of that scale, in everyday life there are many experiences where we just drift and experience an unorganized flow of events, and on the other end we experience events that do have a clear beginning and end but that only mechanically connect the events with one another. Aesthetic experiences exist between those extremes. They have a beginning and an end; they can be uniquely named afterward and in addition the experience has a unity—there is a single quality that pervades the entire experience:

> "An experience has a unity that gives it its name, that meal, that storm, that rupture of a friendship. The existence of this unity is constituted by a single quality that pervades the entire experience in spite of the variation of its constituent parts" (Dewey, 1934/2005).

In such a holistic perspective, it will not make sense to talk about emotions, or the sense of presence as something separate from our embodied experience of being in the world. It is the coming together, the confluence, of humans and technologies that needs to be the focus of interaction design. This aesthetic quality of the whole interaction has been well described in *Technology as Experience* (McCarthy and Wright, 2004; Wright and McCarthy, 2010) where the "felt sense" of experience is foregrounded.

We have also seen that all experiences occur in a place, as to be a person is to be somewhere. Places require movement and this too needs design. We have seen Benford and colleagues (Benford et al., 2011) develop the concept of "interaction trajectories" in their analysis of their experiences with a number of mixed reality, pervasive experiences (Section 7.3). We have also discussed customer journeys (Chapter 1) and ideas of navigation of information space (Section 8.2). With this view, cognitive engineering gives way to a more design-oriented discipline akin to architecture or interior design. These disciplines emphasize flow and the unfolding of experience. It is the design of people's experiences as they move through environments containing mixed reality, multi-modal interactions over time that needs to be foregrounded in the design of places for experience. Navigation of information space, or an interaction trajectory, emphasizes the importance of the body as a central component of interaction. This brings us back to the medium of interaction discussed in Chapter 2 and how to understand navigation in blended spaces (Section 9.3).

The third contribution to designing for the new places for experience comes from conceptual blending theory. In Imaz and Benyon (2007) we laid out some early ideas on how principles from conceptual blending can be applied to design. We emphasized how the bodily basis of thought underlies how people make sense of the world (Section 2.1) and how a number of principles of blends—the integration principle, web and unpacking, topology—can be applied to interaction design. The overall message is to "design at the human scale." In short, design for human experiences and human ways of understanding.

10.2   BLENDED PLACES

We have seen how to design for experience by thinking about how the physical and digital spaces are blended together and a new conceptual space is created in the blend. This creates a new social space. Designers need to consider how social relations will be affected by their designs. We have also seen how people navigate the information space moving through their interactions with physical and digital information artifacts. From our Pact analysis we know that these spaces are directed at people undertaking some activities in some domain in a variety of contexts. We can summarize the design advice by looking at the main types of space that make up the blended places.

10.2.1 DESIGNING THE PHYSICAL SPACE

The design of physical space draws upon the disciplines of architecture and interior design and an understanding of social psychology. The physical space comes with the social expectations of people concerning behaviors and at the same time the physical space will help to shape those behaviors. The physical space allows for interaction between people through touch, proximity, hearing and visual perception. The physical space influences many aspects of the experience such as territory, awareness, control, interaction and transitions (Tacit).

10.2.2 DESIGNING THE DIGITAL SPACE

The digital space concerns data and how it is structured and stored. It concerns the content that is available and the software that is available to manipulate the content. Digital tools need to be appropriate for the physical space and for the characteristics of the devices that interface with the digital space. Gestures, touch and other forms of physical interaction provide a direct engagement between the physical and the digital. The digital space also describes (part of) the information space where the information architecture is critical to UX.

10.2.3 DESIGNING THE CONCEPTUAL SPACE

In a blended space designers bring together the digital and the physical to produce a new space with its own emergent properties and structure. The conceptual space is where people produce meanings and understand where they can go and what they can do. It is also the space of imagination and make believe. People need to understand the relationships between the physical and digital spaces, their organization and structure, so that they can navigate these spaces. It is through, or in, the conceptual space that people work out roles, task allocation and the social organization of their work and play. This is where they figure out what they need to do and how best to do it conceptualizing the opportunities and reacting to the physical and digital constraints.

10.2.4   DESIGNING THE BLENDED SPACE

By thinking about the three spaces—conceptual, physical and digital—that make up the spaces of interaction, we can sensitize designers to the bigger issues. Interaction designers need to design for space and movement as well as interaction with technology. They need to consider the devices that people will bring with them and how these can be integrated into the whole experience of being in, and working in rooms and other interactive spaces. They need to consider how to keep people connected to their personal digital spaces while working and collaborating in shared spaces. The blended space coupled with the rest of the information space and the social space will bring about new blended places for experience.

10.2.5   DESIGNING FOR NAVIGATION

Analogue and digital media are mixed in different ways and need to be managed and interchanged. Digital content is spread across different devices connected through networks into digital ecologies. People have to traverse this information space to explore and discover content, to retrieve particular pieces of content and to understand the objects in the space and what they have to offer. They will also be moving through a physical space. Designers need to design to support the navigation of spaces and the movement between physical and digital spaces.

10.2.6   SUMMARY

Design guidelines for blended spaces come from the principles of designing with blends (Imaz and Benyon, 2007). These concern understanding the correspondences between physical and digital spaces, focusing on the ontology, topology, volatility and agency in the spaces. Design for suitable transitions between the physical and digital spaces and design at a human scale. Designers need to make people aware that there is digital content nearby, to steer them to that content and to enable them to effortlessly access and interact with the content. Designers need to create narratives that direct people through the different spaces and that exploit the characteristics of the physical and digital spaces. Designers should aim to avoid sudden jumps or abrupt changes that will lead to breaks in presence. They should aim for multi-layered, multi-media experiences that weave threads of the physical and the digital into blended fabric for people to engage with. Designers of blended places need to be clear and explicit as to the type of experience they are trying to design for and what features of the spaces they expect to produce feelings of presence.

10.3 CHANGING PLACES

In the new hybrid, blended spaces and environments where digital images commingle with real objects the sense of presence will become increasingly multi-dimensional and distributed. You may feel closely in touch with someone who is miles away at the same time as feeling attachment to the place you are occupying. Simply putting on a pair of glasses will soon take people into a blended space with interactive digital content incorporated into their being instead of it being mediated by a tablet device. Implants will be incorporated into people enabling them to directly sense new aspects of the world such as radiation, air quality and so on.

A European research program on human-computer confluence has recently finished and has brought many ideas and concepts to bear on understanding future places for experience. Contributions from design, neuroscience, psychology, art, pervasive computing and related disciplines have been gathered into a book of visions of these new places (HC2, 2014). There will be new forms of collective attention. Synesthetic experiences will allow new ways of perceiving. Taste and smell will become part of the digital space. The massive amounts of data now being gathered and processed will impact the human condition. Cities being covered in layers of technologies and digital and information spaces will fundamentally change the nature of being. People will add layers of their own experiences, as sound, photos, video and animations onto physical locations. Curators will bring historical artifacts and experiences into the present day. Artists will create fantastic displays with mixed reality spaces. Interaction designers would do well to look at these visions to see what future interactions will bring.

Hiroshi Ishii has been looking at the relationship between atoms and bits for over twenty years through a large number of projects. His current vision is for "radical atoms," which he describes: "we envision that Radical Atoms will provide sensing, actuation, and communication capabilities at the molecular level. Advances in material science, nanotechnology, and self-organizing micro-robotic technology are opening new possibilities to materialize the vision of Radical Atoms." (Ishii, et al., 2012). In this paper Ishii and his colleagues explore fictional materials that would allow the bringing together of atoms and bits allowing people to physically interact directly with digital content and for the information content to be consistently represented in the physical state of the material. Such materials, where nanotechnologies form an integral part of the interaction are not here yet, but they are not far away. Taken with Mikael Wiberg's notion of texture and his more radical view that the distinction between atoms and bits is not longer useful (Wiberg and Robles, 2010), we see blended places contributing to the next period of interaction design.

10.4 CONCLUSION

Heidegger's maxim that "We are involved with the world, places disclose things to us" needs to take on board the technology that is now so embedded in our experiences, and the social nature of interaction. Richard Coyne (Coyne, 2010) proposes that people's use of pervasive digital media enables them to make incremental changes to their world, something he describes as the tuning of place.

In taking a spatial view of the interaction of people in the technology rich world in which we exist we hope to have opened up a useful way of looking at interaction design in the age of pervasive computing. We started off with the idea that people exist inside media, thousands of them at any one time. The ontology of this people-medium mix is people, activities, contexts and technologies, Pacts.

Making meaning in the world depends on interactive experiences. Our semiotics is not to do with the transmission of signs it is to do with how signs function in Pacts as interactive constructs and how people use interactivity to enable them to think, act, feel and have intentions.

We have also explored the different spaces that make up these new places for interaction and experience; the physical space, digital space, information space, conceptual space, social space and blended physical-digital space. Each of these brings its own constraints and affordances that need to be woven into places for experience. But of course things do not stand still and the new wave of technology is coming: wearable devices, clothing, implants, personal sensors and ambient environments with embedded sensors and actuators. Our media will expand and our extensions will take us into new places and new experiences.

References

Ackerman, M. (2000). The Intellectual Challenge of CSCW: The Gap Between Social Require-
    ments and Technical Feasibility. *Human-Computer Interaction* 15(2), 179–203. DOI:
    10.1207/S15327051HCI1523_5. 64

Alexander, C. (1979). *The Timeless Way of Building*. Oxford University Press. 32, 33

Arthur, P. and Passini, R. (2002). *Wayfinding*. Focus Strategic Communications. 22

Bannon, L. (2011). Reimagining HCI: Toward a More Human-Centered Perspective. *Interactions*,
    18(4), 50–57. DOI: 10.1145/1978822.1978833. 1

Baillie, L. and Benyon, D. (2008). Place and Technology in the Home. *Computer Supported Cooper-
    ative Work* 17(2–3) 227–256. DOI: 10.1007/s10606-007-9063-2. 66

Bardzell, J. (2011). Interaction Criticism. *Interacting with Computers* 23. DOI: 10.1016/j.int-
    com.2011.07.001. 23

Benford, S. and Fahlén, L. (1993). A Spatial Model of Interaction in Large Virtual Environ-
    ments. Presented at the ECSCW'93: *Proceedings of the Third Conference on European
    Conference on Computer-Supported Cooperative Work*, Kluwer Academic Publishers. DOI:
    10.1007/978-94-011-2094-4_8. 41

Benford, S., Lindt, I., Crabtree, A., Flintham, M., Greenhalgh, C., Koleva, B., et al. (2011). Creat-
    ing the Spectacle. *ACM Transactions on Computer-Human Interaction* 18(3), 1–28. DOI:
    10.1145/1993060.1993061. 67, 69, 82, 98

Benyon, D. R. (1998). Cognitive Ergonomics as Navigation in Information Space *Ergonomics* 41(2),
    153–156. 51

Benyon, D. R. (2001). The New HCI? Navigation of Information Space. *Knowledge-based Systems*
    14(8), 425–430. DOI: 10.1016/S0950-7051(01)00135-6. 51

Benyon, D. R. (2005). Information Space. In Ghaoul, C. (ed.) *The Encyclopedia of Human-Computer
    Interaction*. DOI: 10.4018/978-1-59140-562-7.ch053. 51

Benyon, D. R. (2006). Navigating Information Space: Website design and lessons from the built
    environment. *Psychology* 4(1), 7–24. 49

Benyon, D. R. (2007). Information Architecture and Navigation Design for Websites. In Zaphyris,
    P. and Surinam, K. (eds.), *Human Computer Interaction Research in Web Design and Eval-
    uation*, 163–182. DOI: 10.4018/978-1-59904-246-6. 49

Benyon, D. R., Smyth, M., McCall, R., O'Neill, S., and Carroll, F. (2005.) The Place Probe: Exploring a Sense of Place in Real and Virtual Environments. *Presence: Teleoperators and virtual environments* 15(6) 668–688. DOI: 10.1162/pres.15.6.668. 31, 32

Benyon, D., and Höök, K. (1997). Navigation in Information Spaces: Supporting the Individual. In *Human-Computer Interaction: INTERACT'97*, Chapman and Hall. DOI: 10.1007/978-0-387-35175-9_7. 70

Benyon, D. R. and Mival, O. (2014). Designing Blended Spaces for Collaboration. In Gagglioli, A., Fersha, A., Riva, G. Dunne, S. and Viud-Delmon, I. (eds.) *Human-Computer Confluence* Versita Open. 79

Bertin, J. (1981). *Graphics and Graphic Information Processing*. Walter de Gruyter. DOI: 10.1515/9783110854688. 22

Blackwell, A. F. (2006). The Reification of Metaphor as a Design Tool. *ACM Transaction on Computer Human Interaction* 13(4) 490–530. DOI: 10.1145/1188816.1188820. 57

Blythe, M. A., Monk, A., Overbeeke, L. and Wright, P. (eds.) (2006). *Funology*. Springer. DOI: 10.1007/1-4020-2967-5. 9

Bødker, S. and Klokmose, C. (2012). Dynamics in Artifact Ecologies. *Proceedings of the 7th Nordic Conference on Human-Computer Interaction: Making Sense Through Design*. ACM, 448–457. DOI: 10.1145/2399016.2399085. 40, 55

Bolter, D. and Grusin, R. (2000). *Remediation; Understanding New Media*. MIT Press. 17

Bolter, D. and Gromala, D. (2003). *Windows and Mirrors: Interaction Design, Digital Art, and the Myth of Transparency*. MIT Press. 17

Bullivant, L. (2006). *Responsive Environments: Architecture, Art and Design*. V&A publications. 66

Buxton, W. (2009). Mediaspace—Meaningspace—Meetingspace. In Harrison, S. (ed.) *20 Years of MediaSpace*. Springer. 34, 64

Canter, D. V. (1977). The Psychology of Place. In G. T. Moore and R. W. Marans (eds.), *Advances in Environment, Behavior, and Design*, Vol. 4: Toward the Integration of Theory, Methods, Research, and Utilization. New York: Plenum, 109–147. 1997. 32

Card, S. (2012). Information Visualization. In Jacko, J. (ed.) *The Handbook of HCI*, 3rd edition. CRC Press. DOI: 10.1145/274430.274432. 22, 75

Casey, E. S. (2009). *Getting Back Into Place*. Indiana University Press. xiii, 35

Chalmers, M., Bell, M., Brown, B., Hall, M., Sherwood, S., and Tennent, P. (2005). Gaming on the Edge: Using Seams in Ubicomp Games (306–309). *ACE '05: Proceedings of the 2005*

ACM SIGCHI International Conference on Advances in computer entertainment technology. DOI: 10.1145/1178477.1178533. 40

Checkland, P. (1999). *Systems Thinking, Systems Practice.* Wiley. 8

Clark, A. (2008). *Supersizing the Mind: Embodiment, Action, and Cognitive Extension* (2008). DOI: 10.1111/j.1467-9213.2010.660_10.x. 20

Clark, A. and Chalmers (1998). The Extended Mind. Reprinted in *The Philosopher's Annual vol. XXI–1998* (Ridgeview). 20

Coughlan, T., Collins, T. D., Adams, A., Rogers, Y., Haya, P. A., and Martín, E. (2012). The Conceptual Framing, Design, and Evaluation of Device Ecologies for Collaborative Activities. *International Journal of Human Computer Studies*, 70(10), 765–779. DOI: 10.1016/j. ijhcs.2012.05.008. 40

Coyne, R. (2010). *The Tuning of Place.* MIT Press (MA). 102

Couldry, N. and McCarthy, A. (eds.) (2004). *MediaSpace: Place Scale and Culture in a Media Age.* Routledge. 16, 17

Crabtree, A. and Rodden, T. (2008). Hybrid Ecologies: Understanding Cooperative Interaction in Emerging Physical-Digital Environments. *Personal and Ubiquitous Computing* 12(7). DOI: 10.1007/s00779-007-0142-7. 40

Cullen, G. (1964). *The Concise Townscape.* Van Rostrand. 32, 72

de Certeau, Michael. (1984). *Walking in the City. In the Practice of Everyday Life.* University of California Press. 30, 69

de Saussure, F. (2013). *Course in General Linguistics.* Columbia University Press. 22

de Souza, C. S. (2005). *The Semiotic Engineering of Human-computer Interaction.* MIT Press. DOI: 10.1016/j.intcom.2005.01.007. 22

Dennett, D. C. (1996). *Kinds Of Minds.* Hachette UK. DOI: 10.1016/S0307-4412(97)84464-0. 54

Dewey, J. (1934/2005). *Art as Experience.* Penguin. 5, 98

Diaper, D., and Stanton, N. (2003). *The Handbook of Task Analysis for Human-Computer Interaction.* CRC Press. 7

Dix, A., Rodden, T., Davies, N., Trevor, J., Friday, A., and Palfreyman, K. (2000). Exploiting Space and Location as a Design Framework for Interactive Mobile Systems. *Transactions on Computer-Human Interaction* 7(3), 285–321. DOI: 10.1145/355324.355325. xiii. 39, 41

Dourish, P. (2004). *Where the Action Is.* MIT Press. 21

Dourish, P. (2006). Re-Space-ing Place. Presented at the *CSCW 20th Anniversary Conference*, New York, New York: ACM Press. DOI: 10.1145/240080.240193. 29

Dourish, P., and Bell, G. (2007). The Infrastructure of Experience and the Experience of Infrastructure: Meaning and Structure in Everyday Encounters with Space. *Environment and Planning B: Planning and Design* 34(3), 414–430. DOI: 10.1068/b32035t. xiii, 40, 61, 66

Dörk, M., Carpendale, S., and Williamson, C. (2011). The Information Flaneur: A Fresh Look at Information Seeking (1215–1224). Presented at the *CHI '11: Proceedings of the SIG-CHI Conference on Human Factors in Computing Systems*, New York, New York. DOI: 10.1145/1978942.1979124. xiii, 46

Downs, R. and Stea, D. (1973). Cognitive Representations. In Downs, R. and Stea, D. (eds.) *Image and Environment*. Aldine. 71

Eco, U. (1976). *A Theory of Semiotics*. Indiana University Press. 23

Eco, U. (1997). *Kant and the Platypus*. Harcourt. 57

Fauconnier, G. and Turner, M. (2002). *The Way We Think*. Basic Books. 58

Floridi, L. (2008). The Method of Levels of Abstraction. *Minds and Machines* 18 (3) 303–329. DOI: 10.1007/s11023-008-9113-7. 8

Floridi, L. (2007). The Philosophy of Presence: From Epistemic Failure to Successful Observation. *Presence: Teleoperators and Virtual Environments* 14(6), 656–667. 2007. DOI: 10.1162/105474605775196553. 25

Floridi, L. (2014). *The Fourth Revolution*. Oxford University Press. xiv

Forrlizzi, J. (2007). The Product Ecology: Understanding Social Product Use and Supporting Design Culture. *International Journal of Design* 2(1).61

Garrett, J. J. (2010). *Elements of User Experience*, Pearson Education. DOI: 10.1111/j.1948-7169.2006.tb00027.x. 74

Gibson, J. J. (1979). *The Ecological Approach To Visual Perception*. Psychology Press. 20 ,24

Gibson, W. (1984). *Neuromancer*. HarperCollins UK. 1

Green, T. R. G. and Benyon, D. R. (1996). The Skull Beneath the Skin: Entity-Relationship Models of Information Artifacts. *International Journal of Human-Computer Studies*, 44(6). DOI: 10.1006/ijhc.1996.0034. 47

Gruber, T. R. (1995). Toward Principles for the Design of Ontologies Used for Knowledge Sharing. *International Journal of Human-Computer Studies* 43(5–6). DOI: 10.1006/ijhc.1995.1081. 49

Gruszka, A., Matthews, G., and Szymura, B. (2010). *Handbook of Individual Differences in Cognition.* Springer Science and Business Media. DOI: 10.1007/978-1-4419-1210-7. 69

Gustafson, P. (2001). Meanings of Place: Everyday Experience and Theoretical Conceptualizations, *Journal of Environmental Psychology* 21, 5–16. 2001. DOI: 10.1006/jevp.2000.0185. 31

Hall, E. (1969). *The Hidden Dimension.* Doubleday.

Harrison, S. and Dourish, P. (1996). Re-Place-ing Space (pp. 67–76). Presented at the *CSCW Conference Computer Supported Collaborative Work.* DOI: 10.1145/240080.240193. 29

Hassenzahl, M. (2010). *Experience Design: Technology for All the Right Reasons.* Morgan and Claypool. DOI: 10.2200/S00261ED1V01Y201003HCI008. 9, 12

Haugeland, J. (1995). Mind Embodied and Embedded. In Y. Houng and J. Ho (eds.), *Mind and Cognition.* Taipei: Academia Sinica. 20

HC2 (2014). Human-Computer Confluence website retrieved from http://hcsquared.eu/hc2-visions-book 20.08.14. 101

Heidegger, M. (2010). *Being and Time.* SUNY Press. 27

Hillier B. and J. Hanson J. (1984). *The Social Logic of Space.* Cambridge University Press. 33

Höök, K., Benyon, and Munro, A. J. (2003). *Designing Information Spaces: The Social Navigation Approach.* Springer. 56, 73

Hornecker, E. and Buur, J. (2006). Getting a Grip on Tangible Interaction: A Framework on Physical Space and Social Interaction, *Proceedings of CHI 2006.* ACM Press. DOI: 10.1145/1124772.1124838. 67

Hoshi, K., Öhberg, F., and Nyberg, A. (2011). Designing Blended Reality Space: Conceptual Foundations and Applications. *Proceedings of British HCI Conference.* 80

Hurtienne, J., Israel, J. H., and Weber, K. (2008). Cooking up Real-World Business Applications Combining Ohysicality, Digitality, and Image Schemas TEI '08. *Proceedings of the 2nd International Conference on Tangible and Embedded Interaction.* DOI: 10.1145/1347390.1347443. 20, 56

Hurtienne, J., Stößel, C., and Weber, K. (2009). Sad Is Heavy and Happy is Light. *Proceedings of the 3rd International Conference on Tangible and Embedded Interaction.* ACM. DOI: 10.1145/1517664.1517686.

Hurtienne, J. and Israel J. (2013). PIBA-DIBA or How to Blend the Digital with the Physical. *Proceedings of CHI 2013 workshop.*

Husserl, E. (1970). *The Crisis of European Sciences and Transcendental Phenomenology: An Introduction to Phenomenological Philosophy.* 6

Hutchins, E. (1996). *Cognition in the Wild*. Bradford Books. DOI: 10.1207/s15327884mca0301_5. 20

Hutchins, E. (2005). Material Anchors for Conceptual Blends. *Journal of Pragmatics* 37(10), 1555–1577. DOI: 10.1016/j.pragma.2004.06.008. 58

Hutchins, E. (2010). Cognitive Ecology. *Topics in Cognitive Science* 2, 705–715. DOI: 10.1111/j.1756-8765.2010.01089.x. 24

Imaz, M. and Benyon. (2007). *Designing with Blends: Conceptual Foundations of Human–Computer Interaction and Software Engineering*. MIT Press. 56, 80, 98, 100

IJsselsteijn, W.A. and Riva, G. (2003). Being There: The Experience of Presence in Mediated Environments. In: Riva, G., Davide, F., and IJsselsteijn, W.A. (eds.), *Being There—Concepts, Effects and Measurements of User Presence in Synthetic Environments*. IOS Press. 26

Ingold, T. (2000). *The Perception of the Environment*. Psychology Press. DOI: 10.4324/9780203466025. 24

Ingold, T. (2007). *Lines a Brief History*. Routledge. xiii

Ingold, T. (2009). Bindings Against Boundaries: Entanglements of Life in an Open World. *Environment and Planning A*. DOI: 10.1068/a40156. 24

Ishii, H. Lakatos, D., Bonanni, L. and Labrune, J-P (2012). Radical Atoms. *Interactions* XiX.1. 101

Ishii, H. and Ullmer, B. (1997). Tangible Bits. In *Proceedings of CHI 97*. (234–241). ACM Press. DOI: 10.1145/258549.258715. 79

Jetter, H.-C. (2012). Blended Interaction—Toward a Framework for the Design of Interactive Spaces, *Proceedings of Designing Collaborative Spaces workshop at AVI 2012*. 79

Jordan, P. W. (2003). *Designing Pleasurable Products*. CRC Press. 9, 11

Johnson-Laird, M. (1983). *Mental Models. Towards a Cognitive Scinece of Language, Inference and Consciousness* Harvard University Press. 53

Jorgensen B. S. and Stedman, R. C. (2001). Sense of Place as an Attitude: Lakeshore Owners Attitudes toward their Properties. *Journal of Environmental Psychology* 21, 233–248. 2001. DOI: 10.1006/jevp.2001.0226. 31

Jung, H., Stolterman, E., Ryan, W., Thompson, T., and Siegel, M. (2008). Toward a Framework for Ecologies of Artifacts: How Are Digital Artifacts Interconnected within a Personal Life? *Proceedings of NordiCHI '08*. DOI: 10.1145/1463160.1463182. 40

Karapanos, E., Zimmerman, J., Forlizzi, J., and Martens, J.-B. (2009). User Experience over Time: An Initial Framework (729–738). *Presented at the CHI '09*: ACM. DOI: 10.1145/1518701.1518814. 12

Kress, G. R. and van Leeuwen, T. (1996). *Reading Images*. Psychology Press. 22

Lakoff, G. (1997). *Women, Fire and Dangerous Things*. University of Chicago Press. 19, 56

Lakoff, G. and Johnson, M. (1980). *Metaphors We Live By*. University of Chicago Press. 19, 55, 58

Lakoff, G. and Johnson, M. (1999). *Philosophy in the Flesh*. Basic Books. 58

Lazzaro, N. (2012). Why We Play: Affect and the Fun of Games. In Jacko, J. (ed.), *The Handbook of HCI*, 3rd edition. CRC Press. 11

Lefebvre, H. (1991). *The Production of Space*. Blackwell Publishing. 30

Lentini, L. and Decortis, F. (2010). Space and Places: When Interacting with and in Physical Space Becomes a Meaningful Experience. *Personal and Ubiquitous Computing* 14(5), 407–415. DOI: 10.1007/s00779-009-0267-y. 27, 30

Lieberman, H. and Selker, T. (2000). Out of Context: Computer Systems that Adapt to, and Learn from, Context. *IBM Systems Journal* 39(3), 617–632. DOI: 10.1147/sj.393.0617. 43

Löffler, D., Lindner, K., and Hurtienne, J. (2014). Mixing Languages. *Extended Abstracts of CHI 2014*. 56

Lombard, M. and Ditton, T. (1997). At the Heart of It All: The Concept of Presence, *Journal of Computer-Mediated Communication* 3(2). 25

Lynch, K. (1960). *The Image of the City*. MIT Press. 32, 71

Malafouris, L. (2013). *How Things Shape the Mind*. MIT Press. 24, 26

Malpas, J. (1999). *Place and Experience*. Cambridge University Press. DOI: 10.1017/CBO9780511487606. xiii, 30

Marcus, A., 2014. http://www.amanda.com/. 7

Markussen, T. (2009). Bloody Robots as Emotional Design: How Emotional Structures May Change Expectations of Technology Use in Hospitals. *International Journal of Design* 3(2). 80

McCarthy, J. and Wright, P. (2004). *Technology as Experience*. MIT Press. DOI: 10.1145/1015530.1015549. 9, 21, 98

McCullough, M. (1998). *Abstracting Craft*. MIT Press. 10

McCullough, M. (2005). *Digital Ground*. MIT Press. 11, 34, 61

McCullough, M. (2013). *Ambient Commons*. MIT Press. 35

McLuhan, M. (1963). *Understanding Media: the Extensions of Man*. Reprinted in 1994 by MIT Press. xiv, 15

Memarovic, N., Langheinrich, M., and Alt, F. (2012). The Interacting Places Framework: Conceptualizing Public Display Applications that Promote Community Interaction and Place Awareness. *Proceedings of the 2012 International Symposium on Pervasive Displays*. DOI: 10.1145/2307798.2307805. 40

Mennecke, B. E., Triplett, J. L., Hassall, L. M., and Conde, Z. J. (2010). Embodied Social Presence Theory. Presented at the HICSS '10: *Proceedings of the 2010 43rd Hawaii International Conference on System Sciences, IEEE Computer Society*. DOI: 10.1109/HICSS.2010.179. 42

Merleau-Ponty, M. (1962). *Philosophy of Perception*. Routledge. 5, 20, 27

Metz, C. (1974). *Film Language*. OUP. 22

Milgram K. and Kishino, P. (1994). A Taxonomy of Mixed Reality Visual Displays, *IEICE Transactions on Information Systems E77-D* (12), 1321–1329. 79

Mival, O. and Benyon, D. (2013). Designing an interactive Collaborative Environment. *CHI 2013 Blended Spaces Workshop*.

Monk, A. (2008). *Common Ground*. Morgan and Claypool. DOI: 10.2200/S00154ED1V01Y-200810HCI001. 62

Norberg-Schulz, C. (1980). *Genius Loci*. Rizzoli. 32, 71

Norman, D. A. (2004). *Emotional Design*. Basic Books. 11

O'Hara, K., Kjeldskov, J., and Paay, J. (2011). Blended Interaction Spaces for Distributed Team Collaboration. *ACM Transactions on Computer-Human Interaction* 18(1), 1–28. DOI: 10.1145/1959022.1959025. 65, 79

O'Keefe, B., Benyon, D. R., Chandwani, G., Menon, M., Duke, R. II (2014). A Blended Space for Heritage Storytelling. *Proceedings of the British HCI Conference BCS-HCI* 14. 89

O'Neil, S. (2008). *Interactive Media: The Semiotics of Embodied Interaction*. Springer. DOI: 10.1007/978-1-84800-036-0. 16, 22

Passini, R. (1992). *Wayfinding in Architecture*. Wiley Inc. 71

Peltonen, P., Kurvinen, E., Salovaara, A., Jacucci, G., Ilmonen, T., Evans, J., et al. (2008). It"s Mine, Don't Touch! *Proceedings of CHI 2008*. ACM Press. 64

Polyani, M. (1983). *The Tacit Dimension*. University of Chicago Press. 54

Pylyshyn, Z. W. (1986). *Computation and Cognition*. Bradford Books. 54

Rasmussen, J. (1986). *Information Processing and Human-Machine Interaction*. Elsevier Science Ltd. 55

Relph, E. (1976). *Place and Placelessness*. Pion. 31

Riva, G., Waterworth, J. A., and Waterworth, E. L. (2004). The Layers of Presence: A Bio-Cultural Approach to Understanding Presence in Natural and Mediated Environments. *Cyberpsychology and Behavior* 7(4) 402–416. DOI: 10.1089/cpb.2004.7.402. 25

Riva, G., Waterworth, J. A., Waterworth E. L., and Mantovani, F. (2011). From Intention to Action: The Role of Presence. *New Ideas in Psychology* 29 (1), 24–37. DOI: 10.1016/j.newideapsych.2009.11.002. 26

Rogers, Y. (2006). Moving on From Weiser's Vision of Calm Computing: Engaging Ubicomp Experiences. *Presented at the UbiComp'06*: Springer-Verlag. DOI: 10.1007/11853565_24. 40, 65

Rohrer, T. (2005). Image Schemata in the Brain. In Hampe, B. and Grady, J. (eds.) *From Perception to Meaning*. Mouton de Gruyer. DOI: 10.1515/9783110197532.2.165. 19

Rosch, E. (1976). Basic Objects in Natural Categories. *Cognitive Psychology* 8, 382–440. DOI: 10.1016/0010-0285(76)90013-X. 57

Saffer, D. (2013). *Microinteractions*. O'Reilly Media, Inc. 6

Schön, D. A. (1983). *The Reflective Practitioner*. Basic Books. 2

Scott, S. D., and Carpendale, S. (2010). Theory of Tabletop Territoriality. In *Human-Computer Interaction Series*. Springer London. DOI: 10.1007/978-1-84996-113-4_15. 64

Shedroff, N. (2009). *Experience Design, a Manifesto for the Creation of Experiences*. New Riders. 9, 10

Sowa, J. F. (1995). Top-Level Ontological Categories. *International Journal of Human-Computer Studies*, 43(5–6). DOI: 10.1006/ijhc.1995.1068. 49

Spiegelberg, H. (1956). Husserl's and Peirce's Phenomenologies: Coincidence or Interaction? *Philosophy and Phenomenological Research* 17(2) 164–185. DOI: 10.2307/2104214. 21

Stolterman, E. and Wiberg, M. (2010). Concept-Driven Interaction Design Research. *Human-Computer Interaction*, 25(2) 95–118. DOI: 10.1080/07370020903586696. xiii

Terrenghi, L., Quigley, A., and Dix, A. (2009). A Taxonomy for and Analysis of Multi-Person-Display Ecosystems. *Personal and Ubiquitous Computing* 13(8). DOI: 10.1007/s00779-009-0244-5. xiii, 39

Tuan, Li-Fu (1977). *Space and Place*. University of Minnesota Press. 31

Turner P. and Turner (2006). Place, Sense of Place, and Presence. *Presence: Teleoperators and Virtual Environments* 15(2) 204–217. DOI: 10.1162/pres.2006.15.2.204. 31

Turner, P. (2013). *How We Cope with Digital Technology*. Morgan and Claypool. DOI: 10.2200/S00519ED2V01Y201307HCI018. 54, 59

Tversky, B. (2003). Navigating by Mind and by Body. *Spatial Cognition*, 2685. DOI: 10.1007/3-540-45004-1_1. 70

Urry, J. (2013). *The Tourist Gaze*. Sage. 35

Veerapen, M. (2011). How Did the Computer Disappear?: HCI during the *Experience of Second Life Proceedings of the 2011 ISPR Presence Conference*, ACM. 42

Venkatesh, A., Kruse, E. and Shih, E. (2003). The Networked Home: An Analysis of Current Developments and Future Trends. *Cognition, Technology and Work* 5(1) 23–32. DOI: 10.1007/s10111-002-0113-8. 66

Vicente, K. J. and Rasmussen, J. (1992). Ecological Interface Design: Theoretical Foundations. *IEEE Transactions on Systems, Man, and Cybernetics* 22(4), 589–606. DOI: 10.1109/21.156574. 55

Wagner, I., Broll, W., Jacucci, G., Kuutii, K., McCall, R., Morrison, A., et al. (2009). On the Role of Presence in Mixed Reality. *Presence: Teleoperators and Virtual Environments* 18(4). DOI: 10.1162/pres.18.4.249. 81

Weiser, M. (1991). The Computer of the 21st Century. *Scientific American* 265(9) 66–75. 39

Weiser, M. and Seeely Brown, J. (1995). Designing Calm Technology. http://www.ubiq.com/hypertext/weiser/calmtech/calmtech.htm, accessed July 1, 2014. 39

Wiberg, M. and Robles, E. (2010). Computational Compositions: Aesthetics, Materials, and Interaction Design. *International Journal of Design* 4(2), 65–76. 101

Winograd, T. (1996). *Bringing Design to Software*. Addison-Wesley. 1, 2

Witmer, B. G. and Singer, M. J. (1998). Measuring Presence in Virtual Environments: A Presence Questionnaire. *Presence: Teleoperators and Virtual Environments* 7(3). DOI: 10.1162/105474698565686. 25

Wright, P. C. and McCarthy, J. (2010). *Experience-Centered Design*. Morgan and Claypool. DOI: 10.2200/S00229ED1V01Y201003HCI009. 9, 98

Zimmerman, J. (2009). Designing for the Self: Making Products that Help People Become the Person They Desire To Be (395–404). Presented at the *CHI '09: Proceedings ACM*. DOI: 10.1145/1518701.1518765. 12

Author Biography

David Benyon is Professor of Human-Computer Systems and head of the Center for interaction Design at Edinburgh Napier University in Scotland, UK. He obtained an MSc in Computing and Cognition and completed his Ph.D. in 1993 on the subject of Intelligent User Interfaces. Prof. Benyon has written or edited 11 books on Human-Computer Interaction and Interaction Design and published over 150 academic papers including 30 journal papers. Over the last 7 years he has obtained significant funding to support his research including six major EC grants. Prof. Benyon is a member of several professional societies and is on the editorial board for the journals *Knowledge-Based Systems* and *International Journal of People-Oriented Programming*. He has authored a major textbook in the area entitled *Designing Interactive Systems* (the 3rd edition was published in 2013). One of the key books published by Prof. Benyon is *Designing with Blends* (with Manuel Imaz, MIT Press, 2007) which has helped to introduce conceptual blending to the interaction design community.

Printed in the United States
by Baker & Taylor Publisher Services